"In *Redefining Diversity*, Dr. Roosevelt Thomas provides a powerful new way to address diversity of all types in the workplace. The insights in this book will be helpful for corporate managers in dealing with the challenges and opportunities presented by diversity issues."

—E. R. Brooks, Chairman & CEO,
Central and South West Corporation

"I now have an understanding of diversity that I can articulate to others. It goes well beyond race and gender and is inclusive rather than exclusive. It all comes together now!"

—William J. Mossett, Vice President & Director,
Employee Relations & Diversity, SmithKline Beecham

"*Redefining Diversity* takes the concept of diversity beyond the work force to the full scope of the enterprise. One will look at business issues in a different light and see solutions and opportunities that were obscured by 'traditional' thinking. With his diversity paradigm, Roosevelt Thomas shows how managing diversity creates competitive advantage and bottom line results."

—Jack Koraleski, Executive Vice President,
Finance & Information Technologies,
Union Pacific Railroad Company

"A must-read for every corporation that expects to prosper as we turn the century. It gives us a new understanding of a key global competitive advantage."

—Worth Loomis, Former President,
The Dexter Corporation

Redefining DIVERSITY

R. Roosevelt Thomas, Jr.

Author of *Beyond Race and Gender*

amacom
American Management Association

New York • Atlanta • Boston • Chicago • Kansas City • San Francisco • Washington, D.C.
Brussels • Mexico City • Tokyo • Toronto

Library of Congress Cataloging-in-Publication Data

Thomas, R. Roosevelt.
    Redefining diversity / R. Roosevelt Thomas, Jr.
        p.   cm.
    Includes bibliographical references and index.
    ISBN 0-8144-0228-3
    1. Diversity in the workplace. 2. Strategic planning.
    3. Organizational effectiveness. I. Title.
    HF5549.5.M5T464   1996
    658.3'041—dc20   96-1867
                                                  CIP

Printing number

10   9   8   7   6   5   4   3

This book is dedicated to
my wife, **Ruby**
my mother, **Icye Potts Thomas**

Contents

Foreword

by John F. Smith, Jr.,
Chairman & CEO, General Motors Corp.

When we at General Motors began listening to Roosevelt
Thomas speak about managing diversity and how this concept would help us move beyond the legal requirements of
and thinking about affirmative action, I believed that we were
at the beginning of a journey that would eventually lead us
beyond just issues in the workplace.

Now that we are on that journey, I remain more convinced than ever that managing our diverse workforce is both
the right thing to do and a competitive business strategy. This
breakthrough book confirms my conviction.

In addition to offering fresh insights on managing workforce diversity, Roosevelt Thomas opens our minds to a new
understanding of *diversity* itself. Defining *diversity* as any collective mixture characterized by differences and similarities,
Thomas contends that managers can view and interpret
many of today's business challenges and opportunities as
diversity mixtures. Thus, diversity serves as a lens through
which they can frame such issues as mergers or joint
ventures, cross-functional synergy efforts, coordination of
multiple lines of business, globalism, learning, and the management of change.

In this stimulating book, Thomas also probes behind the
familiar labels of affirmative action, understanding differences, and Managing Diversity and develops and offers a set
of action options that can be used regardless of the nature of

the mixture in question. This set of options gives managers a straightforward framework for thinking and acting.

Paralleling the spirit of Thomas's ideas, we have expanded Managing Diversity at GM to four key areas of our business: human resources, marketing, minority supplier development, and community relations. As a global employer, we want to build a supportive work environment where every one of our employees has the opportunity to contribute—and has the desire to contribute. Our objective is total employee enthusiasm.

Our commitment to diversity does not end at our door. It includes our dealerships, our suppliers, and the many communities where we operate. We believe that Managing Diversity will impact our performance in the areas of minority supplier development and minority purchases. GM is committed to placing more business in the minority supplier community in an effort to help new businesses grow through the development of sound business plans and the execution of programs aimed at improving quality, price, and service. It is our future as well.

Roosevelt Thomas has described General Motors' work under the umbrella of Managing Diversity as "pioneering." We know it is the most difficult, important work we have undertaken. Certainly, when we began this journey, we had no vision of ourselves as pioneers. The road we have been traveling is fraught with detours and an occasional pothole—costs, competition, and "old ways of doing things."

We are not nearly where we need to be; however, I am encouraged by our change progress. The challenge for business is to focus and channel all insight and creativity that comes from a diverse workforce into policies and products that move the entire organization closer to the customer. We do that by Managing Diversity.

Roosevelt Thomas has provided a foundation on which corporations can ground their efforts to address not only workforce diversity, but diversity of all kinds. For this we are indebted to him.

Preface

Language is a marvelous thing. It both mirrors and leads our collective thinking, changing to reflect changes in our culture and at the same time nudging those changes forward. This dynamic, organic quality of language is, in a way, responsible for the ideas at the heart of this book.

In recent years, the work I have done has been linked with the word *diversity*. But what we mean by that word has changed, and still is changing—and what I mean by it has changed too. And it is this new (perhaps old) meaning, with all its ramifications for business leaders, that I address in this book.

At one time *diversity* simply meant variety, the existence of multiple versions of the thing in question. In the last decade or so in the business world it has been applied mostly to personnel issues. Despite the protests of a few of us who have always interpreted the word more broadly, it has come to be a shorthand descriptor for a workforce made up of people from several racial and cultural groups. As business organizations began to develop specific human resources programs under the label of "affirmative action" or "understanding differences," focused on employees who were in some way different from the main group, the meaning subtly shifted. *Diversity* became a more delicate way of saying "minorities." In some situations, it has narrowed down even further, to a sort of code word for "African-American"; when certain organizations and certain individuals say "diversity," they really mean "black."

A few years ago, in a book entitled *Beyond Race and Gender: Unleashing the Power of Your Total Work Force by Managing Diversity*, I described a process by which organizations can create an environment that allows all employees of all cultural backgrounds to reach their full potential in pursuit of company objectives. Because creating such an environment is the essence of management, I called this process Managing Diversity.[1]

But no miracles occurred. In spite of the best efforts of people of goodwill, American business organizations are little better equipped today to deal with the fragile threads of a multicultural workforce than they were in earlier days of overt racism and despicable epithets. In this case, language preceded culture: We have changed our vocabulary but not our behavior.

In recent months I have found myself thinking a great deal about this dilemma; it is, after all, the main thrust of my current professional life. Gradually my thoughts coalesced around a structure that provided multiple options for dealing with workforce diversity. That structure, which I call the Diversity Paradigm, is the core of a new Diversity Management process, and it is described in detail in Chapter 2.

The more I worked with this concept, fine-tuning it from many angles, the more I came to believe that it had usefulness far beyond the "personnel" arena most people envision when they hear the word *diversity*. I began to feel certain that the model of options, and the operational rationale on which it rests, could as reasonably provide guidance in many other complex, worrisome, even life-threatening business situations. I also believed, with the sense of excitement known by educators, that it offered a way to increase understanding, to teach the true meaning of diversity.

And so I found myself coming back full circle, semantically speaking. If this model could serve business leaders more broadly than simply with workforce diversity, then it actually addressed a broader definition of *diversity*. And so that word, which once meant "any collection of variables" and then narrowed itself to just "different kinds of people," now had widened out again.

Have we finally reached that place where we can bring our words and our actions into harmony? Can we use diversity, in its broadest sense, to strengthen our organizations in all dimensions, including their human resources? No one can say for sure. But I do know that if we make any progress in the days ahead, it will be because we have found a way, or several ways, to keep our companies from crashing on the rocks while we nurture the potential of all our people and effectively address diversity in whatever form it might arise. For this effort, business leaders may find in this book some fresh ideas.

Acknowledgments

Any progress I have made in understanding diversity and its dynamics can be attributed to the support I have received from many individuals. I wish to acknowledge this assistance.

As has always been the case, my wife Ruby and our children, Shane, April, and Jarred, have been supportive of my efforts to comprehend diversity. Their encouragement has been most meaningful.

Similarly, my mother, Icye P. Thomas and my grandmother, the late Lela M. Potts, have exhibited a spirit of quiet perseverance that has inspired me in my diversity endeavors.

The staff of The American Institute for Managing Diversity (AIMD) has been most helpful in fostering the development of my thinking. In particular, Robert L. Davis, Toni Gregory, Maureen Hunter, Marshall Kaufman, Terri Kruzan, Catherine Ouellette, and Glenda Westbrook read and offered comments on various chapters.

Morehouse College, through the leadership of President-Emeritus Hugh M. Gloster, former President Leroy Keith and current President Walter E. Massey, has fostered the growth and development of AIMD and its efforts to enhance public understanding of diversity. This support has been important to our efforts.

In many, many ways, this book has been facilitated by current and past members of AIMD's Board of Trustees and Advisory Council. These individuals have displayed remarkable wisdom, commitment and energy in support of The Institute's mission.

I acknowledge the work of Harvard University's Paul R. Lawrence and Jay W. Lorsch. Their work in the 1960s and 1970s provided one of my earliest introductions to the concept of diversity. Reviewing their books and articles, I found it interesting to note the centrality of diversity in their thinking. This acknowledgment is appropriate not just because of publishing protocol, but also because it highlights the reality that the concept of diversity historically has been of managerial interest. Often, we act as if diversity had just arrived on the managerial scene. Not true, it has offered challenges and opportunities for some time. In this book, I seek to build on the foundation provided by Lawrence, Lorsch, and others.

I appreciate earlier consulting opportunities provided in the 1970s and 1980s by Delores Brinkley of the YWCA of the U.S.A. and E. Jayne Ross, formerly of CBS. In these settings, I tried out and refined my thoughts on leadership, management, and race and gender diversity. Those refinements are reflected in this book.

The Diversity Colleguim provided the opportunity, forum, and encouragement for the development of my first cut at the "Diversity Paradigm." Contributing as original members of this group were Price M. Cobbs, Jeff Howard, Marilyn French Hubbard, Kenneth Kelly, Vapordeal Sanders, and Marc Wallace.

I owe a special thanks to the many executives and managers who have dialogued with me on the topic of diversity— whether through formal diversity presentations, small group deliberations, or one-on-one conversations. Frequently, these interactions have generated many learnings for me.

I express appreciation to the corporations included as case studies and also to the individuals who facilitated their company's involvement: BellSouth (Gwen Bowie and Janice R. Mann), EDS (Dan Leffel), General Motors (William Brooks and Victoria Jones), Goodyear (Mike Burns and Jesse Williams), and Hallmark (Tom Wright and Mary Towse). These managers made a major contribution to *Refining Diversity*.

Rebecca Boyter, Richard Hadden, and Kathy Lee contributed to the development of the case studies.

I acknowledge Marjorie Woodruff and Maggie Stuckey for their assistance in organizing and editing the manuscript. Shirley Manor, Linda Wilson, Faith Kinard, and Emma Oakley typed the multiple drafts of the book.

As I have come to expect, Adrienne Hickey, senior acquisitions and planning editor, and her AMACOM colleagues have provided friendly, effective, and professional guidance.

To all of the individuals mentioned above, I am most appreciative.

Part One
Building a New Paradigm

1

A New Understanding of Diversity

Imagine sitting at your desk, in your garden, in your favorite chair at home—wherever you do your hard thinking—then pulling out the mental file folder labeled "diversity" and finding there a way to solve problems like these:

- Integrating several lines of business into a strategic whole
- Orchestrating a merger to maximize benefits and minimize hassles
- Finding ways to make total quality a consistent reality
- Managing change so that you improve the health of your organization without killing the patient in the process
- Evaluating various global opportunities and making smart decisions

"But," you may be asking, "what do those things have to do with diversity? I thought diversity was about getting along with people of different backgrounds; our human resources people are working on that now."

In *Beyond Race and Gender* I argued that we needed to expand our understanding of diversity beyond just race and gender;[1] now I believe that we need to expand it much further, beyond the single arena labeled human resources into the entire spectrum of strategic issues that modern corporations face. I believe that if we can open up our sense of what this word *diversity* means, we will find it holds the key to some of our thorniest problems.

Undoubtedly this will require a real stretch for many people. In our society the defining diversity experiences have been racism and sexism. All we know and believe about diversity—for better or worse—has come from our efforts to fight these "isms." Yet those who are willing to make the stretch and learn to recognize diversity in other areas will be rewarded with a management tool of enormous potential.

That is the essence of this book: a new philosophy about what diversity is, and a new process of Diversity Management that can be of benefit in all strategic areas.

Defining *Diversity*

Every decade or so, people who concern themselves with the vigor of U.S. business organizations fasten onto a particular word or phrase that surfaces from a general, wide-ranging issue. For a time, this buzzword is extra hot. It is found in every article and every speech; people of all disciplines hang their theoretical hats from it.

Before long, the word begins to take on a symbolic meaning: It serves as a simple verbal code for the complex problem from which it originated. And then you have a situation where every person in the country (or so it seems) is using this word to designate the more complex situation, but no one is really sure any longer what it actually means. The word itself—a simple building unit of the English language—has taken on surreal proportions.

We have seen this happen recently with the word *diversity*. For the general public it has become verbal shorthand for a workforce that is multiracial, multicultural, and multiethnic—which means that it comes preloaded with people's own individual perceptions and biases.

For those in business organizations whose primary professional concern is the welfare of the employees—the human resources managers—diversity has become a kind of semantic umbrella that encompasses an assortment of programs that emanate from their department: affirmative action, multi-culturalism, understanding differences, and a host of other well-intentioned undertakings. Senior management and managers of other functions tend to use the word more generally, and often more vaguely, but they too are essentially referring to the demographic characteristics of their workforce.

I think it's time to look at *diversity* in a new light.

I have come to believe that by restricting that word only to "people" issues, we have overlooked a powerful, versatile idea and a new tool that can contribute significantly to many problems facing the modern corporation. In this broader vision, *diversity* applies not only to a company's people concerns but to many other critical areas as well.

We need, in short, a new understanding of diversity. Deliberately changing our sense of what something means is never easy. The definition I offer here is only the beginning of what promises to be a long evolutionary effort. In the chapters that follow, it will gradually become clear why I believe this broader definition is an extraordinarily powerful tool, infinitely more valuable to American business than the narrow definition we now acknowledge.

> Diversity refers to *any* mixture of items characterized by differences and similarities.[2]

Simple enough, on the surface. But like many simple notions, its implications are significant. If we are to put it into operation, we must fully understand what it means, from all angles. Let's look a bit more closely.

1. *Diversity is not synonymous with differences, but encompasses differences and similarities.* Because we are so accus-

tomed to thinking of diversity in terms of workforce demographics, and equating it with the minority constituencies in that workforce, we tend to think diversity means the qualities that are different. Therefore, even when people expand the concept of diversity to include the whole range of strategic issues, they still tend to focus on the differences. But the definition that is put forth here includes not only differences but also similarities.

This is a critical distinction. It means that when making managerial decisions, you no longer have the option of dealing only with the differences or similarities present in the situation; instead, you must deal with both simultaneously. You may face many situations where choosing to consider only the differences or only the similarities is a legitimate option, but this is not the same as dealing with diversity.

One way of conceptualizing this is to think in terms of a macro/micro continuum. A micro perspective looks at the individual component and a macro perspective looks at the mixture. To get at the true nature of diversity (comprising differences *and* similarities) requires an ability to assume both perspectives simultaneously; the micro facilitates identification of differences, and the macro enhances the ability to see similarities.

A basketball player who is concerned about her needs rather than the team's needs is taking the micro perspective. On the other hand, a player who thinks primarily of the team's needs while not recognizing individual strengths has the macro perspective. The diversity perspective is seen in the player who simultaneously considers both the micro needs of the individual players (including herself) and the macro needs of the team.

The manager who sees total quality as a self-contained process that can benefit the corporation has a micro perspective. The manager with a macro perspective sees an overall general business process in which total quality is but one option. She operates from a macro level that highlights similarities; to her, all managerial approaches are essentially the same. The manager who simultaneously appreciates total quality and integrates it with other processes represents the diversity perspective. This manager has a working, cohesive sense of the whole and of the parts.

There is no right or wrong here, except in the sense that what is happening in the environment may make one approach more "right" in the circumstances. The driving determinant is whatever is needed to ensure organizational viability.

2. *Diversity refers to the collective (all-inclusive) mixture of differences and similarities along a given dimension.* When you are dealing with diversity, you are focusing on the collective mixture, not just pieces of it.

To highlight this notion of mixture, visualize a jar of red jelly beans; now imagine adding some green and purple jelly beans. Many would believe that the green and purple jelly beans represent diversity. I suggest that diversity instead is represented by the resultant mixture of red, green, and purple jelly beans.

It is easier to see these jelly beans as a metaphor for the company's employees, in other words, for workforce diversity. Of course, it works equally well as a metaphor for any other aspect of the organization that you might be concerned with: It could as easily represent a mixture of product lines, functions, marketing strategies, or operating philosophies. But for the moment let us stay with workforce mixtures, for in this familiar arena we can most clearly see what is the key consideration here: that diversity is all-inclusive.

When faced with a collection of diverse jelly beans, most managers worry about how to handle the last jelly beans added to the mixture. This is not dealing with diversity. The manager who is truly coping with racial diversity is not dealing with blacks, whites, Hispanics, or Asian Americans but rather with the collective mixture. The true meaning of diversity suggests that if you are concerned about racism, you include all races; if you're concerned about gender, you include both genders; or if you're concerned about age issues, you include all age groups. In other words, the mixture is all-inclusive.

3. *The component elements in diversity mixtures can vary, and so a discussion of diversity must specify the dimensions in question.* The components of a diversity mixture can be people, concepts, concrete items, or abstractions.

If you are reflecting on the many ways your employees can vary (by race, gender, age, education, sexual orientation, geographic origin, or tenure with the organization), that's a mixture whose components are people, individuals categorized along multiple dimensions.

But consider your colleague who is struggling to create an environment where various functions (marketing, research, manufacturing, and finance) can do their best work. In that mixture, the components are abstractions known as organizational units or functions. One may argue that functions are composed of individuals, which is true, but the general manager of multiple functions does not experience this as a mixture of people but rather as a mixture of organizational units.

Consider, also, the manager who is simultaneously using multiple approaches for improved effectiveness: reengineering, total quality, participatory management, and management by objectives. This manager is dealing with a set of ideas, a diversity mixture of abstract entities.

So it is no longer sufficient to say "I'm working on diversity issues"; you must also specify which dimension you are dealing with. Otherwise you are very likely to fall into a fruitless discussion of apples and oranges.

Thinking in terms of "diversity mixture" takes practice, especially for those who are accustomed to seeing diversity as something that relates only to the workforce—which is to say, nearly everyone. Expanding the view of what diversity encompasses and what corporate areas it relates to is no small task. But those who make that conceptual leap will be well rewarded.

Therefore, begin now to teach yourself how to evaluate your situation through this new lens called diversity. Can you describe the circumstance in terms of its component parts, parts that are similar in some respects and dissimilar in others? As you continue through the remaining chapters of this book, challenge yourself to get better at recognizing the diversity mixtures in the situations that appear.

The Critical Link Between Diversity and Complexity

Diversity contributes to complexity. Complexity reflects diversity. The two mirror each other.

Complexity is a function of the number of components involved and the degree of variability—how many different elements you have to work with, and how different they are from one another.[3] The same can be said of diversity: The more lines of business you have, the more functions, the more races represented in your workforce, and the greater the differences among them, the greater the diversity.

In sum, where diversity increases, complexity increases; where complexity becomes pronounced, so does diversity. This link between diversity and complexity is critical to the Diversity Management process that is at the heart of this book. Exhibit 1-1 illustrates the relationship between diversity and complexity.

The human brain does not easily process complexity. Few people are comfortable supporting contradictory ideas at the same time. Yet in a business climate where conditions change in a nanosecond time frame and complications grow exponentially, business leaders must do exactly that. Today's managers must juggle demands that only recently they would have thought impossible contradictions: They must simultaneously mass produce and customize, simultaneously wear function and corporate hats, simultaneously think about the present and the future.

Exhibit 1-1. The diversity-complexity relationship.

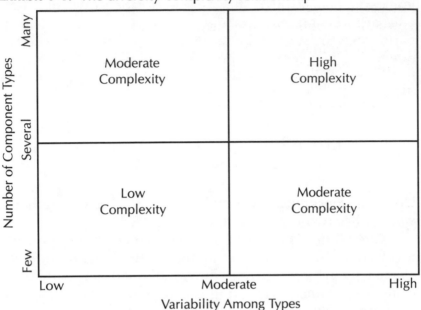

Variability Among Types

Dynamic environments characterized by complexity on all sides, together with the sometimes terrifying need to find new formulas for competitive advantage, are forcing managers to expand their capability to deal with such apparent contradictions. To facilitate that expansion, the approach described in this book—the Diversity Management process—holds profound potential. In short, those who develop skill at understanding and dealing with diversity will also know how to understand and deal with complexity.

A New Tool for Strategic Management

Consider the following circumstances, any one of which, if mismanaged, can bring even the strongest company to near ruin.

- *Workforce diversity.* Today, managers are facing the most diverse workforce ever.[4] Women, minorities, and immigrants are growing in number and playing increasingly important roles; yet managers struggle continually to find vehicles to ensure full use of these employees' potentials.

• *Teaming.* Many corporations are turning to teaming as a strategic structure.[5] Transforming a group of people from different functions and other significant variations into a cohesive, focused unit can be an imposing challenge.

• *Globalism.* As opportunities abroad present themselves, managers must deal with more and more complexity across a wide variety of national situations. This complexity stretches traditional perspectives and structures.[6]

• *Acquisitions and mergers.* American corporations appear to alternate between periods of inclination and disinclination toward acquisitions and mergers, between celebrating the advantages of having variety and emphasizing those associated with sticking to the basic business.[7] They move back and forth between strategies of acquisitions and divestitures, so much so that some managers are now gun-shy and confused.

• *Work/family.* In all kinds of organizations, managers are being asked to accommodate a wider variety of employees' expectations about balance between work and family. In spite of much attention and some progress, the growing consensus is that movement has been too slow.[8]

• *Cross-functional coordination.* Achieving effective collaboration between functions while pushing for excellence in all functions is one of the most difficult of all managerial challenges.[9] We have devoted much time and attention to cross-functional coordination, but it is not getting any easier.

• *Managing change.* Managers who take on the role of change agents find themselves challenging environments that are complex and dynamic and that demand equally dynamic and complex adaptation.[10] But frequently they encounter resistance from colleagues who have difficulty accepting and understanding this complexity. For example: Change agents, by definition, present cutting-edge ideas that have not been quantified. Often their ideas are met with unanswerable questions like these: Do you have numbers to support your propositions? Can you prove what you are recommending will work? Result: stalemate.

What do each of these situations have in common? Each one is dauntingly complex; each one represents a diversity mixture.

Few would argue that they are complex; recognizing them as diversity mixtures takes a bit of practice. Let's take a moment to analyze the ingredients of the mixtures.

With *workforce diversity*, you have a mixture of people who can vary along an infinite number of lines: age, tenure, lifestyle, sexual orientation, education, experience, geographic origin, race, gender—just to name a few possibilities. If you are organizing around *teams*, you have similar concerns: a collection of people who can vary along many dimensions and who probably come from very different operating units in the company.

If *globalism* is your immediate concern, you have to deal with a mixture of nations that have differences and similarities in terms of people, history, culture, religion, politics, technology, priorities, and location.

With *acquisitions and mergers*, you have a mixture of entities that may be different and similar in nature of business, strategy, success factors, vision, mission, technology, culture, financial status, and people.

The range of *work/family* issues represented by your total workforce is growing every day. You have single parents, childless couples, traditional couples with children, and same-sex couples with children. Some of your employees are totally oriented toward work, some are committed primarily to family, and some are actively seeking a balance between work, family, and personal life.

If you are wrestling with the particularly difficult issue of *cross-functional coordination*, you have a mixture of functions that can have similarities and differences regarding tasks, goals, communication patterns, time orientation, people (with all *their* differences and similarities), and culture.

Managing change means dealing with a mixture of quantitative *and* nonquantitative data. This is simply the reality with which you must cope. If people cannot deal with both kinds of data, the change process will be compromised. People who say "I can work only with quantifiable data" are unable to cope with the complexity of the data coming to the organization. In effect, they are saying, "I will make decisions based only on quantitative data, simply because I cannot process other data." This attitude creates a serious handicap for companies that operate in a complex environment that presents both quantitative and qualitative data—which is to say, for almost all companies.

In all these cases, you as the operating manager face fundamental questions:

- How do I create an environment in which all employees and team members, with their diverse backgrounds and work/family parameters, can contribute to their full potential?
- How do I create a global organization that will enable full realization of the corporation's business potential in each country individually and also across the countries collectively?
- How can I weave the acquisition/merger partners into one effective organization?
- Without inappropriately or unnecessarily compromising the integrity of each function, how do I secure the required collaboration and unity of efforts?
- How do I enhance our ability to process diverse, complex data?

A moment's analysis reveals something interesting: Allowing for their slightly different form, these are really all the same question: What can I do about this very complex situation, where some things are the same and other things are different? What course of action can I take that does not alienate one element or another? How do I adapt to our changing environment while staying focused on achieving our corporate objectives? How can I find a way through all these roadblocks and potholes to a reasonable, workable, effective solution?

In the beginning of this chapter, I promised a tool versatile enough to deal with any of these problems. It is also powerful enough to deal with more than one at the same time.

Consider for a moment what that means. If one tool can be brought to bear on a wide range of issues, you immediately have gained two very powerful advantages: economy of learning and synergy. Once you have mastered the use of this tool, you can quickly apply it to other situations; you no longer need to reinvent the wheel for each new problem. What you learn from one situation is an opportunity for leverage in other situations, saving time and avoiding expensive duplications of effort. And you are now in a position to lead an informed, coordinated process that produces change in a more cohesive, efficient manner.

This tool is the Diversity Management process.

The Diversity Management Process

Step 1: Get Clear on the Problem

The first step in solving a problem is to analyze what is happening. What changes are occurring in the environment your company does business in, and how important are they? What do you need to succeed in your organizational mission, and what is interfering with your achieving success? What exactly is the problem?

This is not as easy as it sounds. Being able to see clearly, without prejudgments or personal bias, what is happening while you are in the midst of it is an important skill for managers. Future thinking—being able to understand what you see and project its implications—is one hallmark of leaders.

Step 2: Analyze the Diversity Mixture

The next step is analyze the elements in the set of circumstances you are dealing with. Your goal is to be able to define the situation in terms of a diversity mixture. What are the elements of the mixture at hand? This may be—probably is—a new concept for you. It may be useful to think back to the situations sketched broadly earlier in this chapter—cross-functional coordination, globalism, and the rest—and review the elements of their mixtures.

For example, if your concern is a mixture of product lines, they may be similar (or different) in the mechanisms used to manufacture them, in distribution channels, in profitability ratios, in current or potential customer base, in development costs, in need for consumer advertising, in their position in the product-maturity cycle, in government regulatory requirements, and so on. Forcing yourself to consider all parts of the mixture is a first step in being sure you have covered all the bases when you plan a solution.

Step 3: Check for Diversity Tension

After Step 2, you must ask yourself two questions: Am I seeing tension here as a result of this diversity mixture? And if so, do I need to do anything about it? *Diversity tension* refers to the conflict, stress, and strain associated with the interactions of the elements in the mixture. Tension of some sort often accompanies a diversity mixture—but not always. When it is present, diversity tension is usually easy to spot. It may take different forms, or show itself in varying degrees, but generally we know tension when we see it. The real question is, does it require attention?

Not all tension is bad. "Good" tension produces new ideas, new products, new processes. Good tension acts like fine-grit sandpaper, refining and polishing rough ideas into a gleaming finished product. Tension is a problem only when it interferes with your ability to achieve organizational objectives.

Counterproductive tension is usually obvious. Dysfunctions abound: Interpersonal relationships disintegrate into constant squabbling; petty rivalries between departments end up paralyzing work; functions and work groups that are nominally collaborating are in fact sabotaging each other. Even when goodwill is intact, the complex nature of the situation itself can create tensions that cripple productivity.

Consider the following scenarios.

A DEPARTMENT IN A HIGH-TECH FIRM is called the engineering development department; its task is to convert engineering designs from Research and Development into plans appropriate for Manufacturing. Since most of the company's business calls for customization, this interface process is critical. However, it has also been extremely dysfunctional for a long time: The engineering development department has managed to consistently anger both Manufacturing and Research and Development.

Senior management considered this a serious conflict of personalities and sought to resolve the problem by finding a less cantankerous department head capable of establishing good relations. They went through four new department heads, and each in turn proved incapable of minimizing this conflict. Eventually, the company reportedly went out of business. This failure was caused by many factors, but the continuing conflict surely contributed.[11]

In this case, management recognized the impact that the tension had on the business but misdiagnosed the root cause. They failed to realize that, rather than personalities, they were dealing with a diversity mixture of three work units that differed greatly in many respects. Research and Development staff valued the "science" component of their work and sought scientific excellence regardless of the production implications. Manufacturing focused on the need for effective, economical production runs and often complained that Research and Development sent out unrealistic, unworkable plans. Engineering Development had the impossible task of satisfying both other departments simultaneously. Having misdiagnosed the situation, senior managers were hard pressed to find effective action.

AN INTERFUNCTIONAL TASK FORCE working on strategic planning faced tension emanating from one member. This group had met several times, and at each session this person had taken up much of the time pressing a point of view not understood by his colleagues. Finally, someone spoke up: "The truth is, I'm tired of hearing about this." Another person added, "I'm not sure it makes sense to spend so much time trying to understand your perspective; as a result, we're not dealing with our agenda." As they listened to themselves, it became clear that they were experiencing diversity tension, although they shared a strong common interest in the topic under discussion and were of one mind in other significant ways. The group decided that their goal of productive discussion could not be met by continuing to include this individual, and they asked him to resign from the task force.

A COMPANY WHOSE PRODUCT WAS A COMMODITY had determined that its key success factors were price and customer service. The manufacturing scheduler had the task of scheduling production runs in such a way as to minimize costs and yet allow for customer satisfaction. No matter what she did, either Manufacturing or Sales would be dissatisfied—sometimes both.

Because of the enormous tension generated by these circumstances, management reviewed the situation to see if steps could be implemented to ease the conflict. With the help of a consultant, they concluded that the tension was inescapable and that the company would always have to balance this cost/service question. The scheduler's job was to facilitate this balance on a case-by-case basis.

Note that in this case the company's continued success did not hinge on *eliminating* tension; the prescription was to help everyone understand the tension and the case-by-case problem-solving approach. In particular, participants were encouraged to understand that the tension was not personal.

The important point here is that you need to hone your analytical skills. You need to learn to recognize tension and to be clear on its root causes, on whether it is getting in the way of success, and whether, and how, it is directly linked to the primary problem.

Step 4: Review Action Options

Your task at this point is to dispassionately review what is currently being done to address your primary problems, and decide how well that approach is working. If it is not working well—which is likely if your tension level is high—it's time to try something else.

To help managers find that "something else," I developed the structure called the Diversity Paradigm, which is the heart of the Diversity Management process. The Paradigm presents eight action options, described in detail in the next chapter. Once managers have figured out the essence of the problem, the task is to review the eight options in the light of the particular situation, and choose one (or more) that seems to offer the best hope of solving the problem.

In sum, then, the Diversity Management process consists of these steps:

1. Analyze the circumstances and identify the problem.
2. Identify the diversity mixture at hand; define its ingredients.
3. Determine whether diversity tension is present and, if so, whether it is interfering with success.
4. Review the action options and choose one or more to implement.

2

The Diversity Paradigm: Eight Options for Action

At the core of the Diversity Management process is the Diversity Paradigm; it spells out the action options and defines a system for selecting the appropriate option for a given set of circumstances.

What is a paradigm? Joel Arthur Barker defines it this way: "A paradigm is a set of rules and regulations (written or unwritten) that does two things: (1) it establishes or defines boundaries; and (2) it tells you how to behave inside the boundaries in order to be successful."[1]

A paradigm, therefore, is a way of thinking that facilitates diagnosis, understanding, and action planning. It also provides a way of organizing data, of discovering and recognizing patterns. At a minimum a paradigm concerning diversity should address two fundamental questions:

1. Considering the diversity mixture at hand, what are the available action choices?
2. What are the factors that determine what action is selected?

Eight Action Options

What options are available to managers as they address diversity issues? Essentially, there are eight basic responses (see Exhibit 2-1).[2]

Exhibit 2-1. The Diversity Paradigm's action options.

Option	Description
1. Include/exclude	Include by expanding the number and variability of mixture components. Or exclude by minimizing the number and variability of mixture components.
2. Deny	Minimize mixture diversity by explaining it away.
3. Assimilate	Minimize mixture diversity by insisting that "minority" components conform to the norms of the dominant factor.
4. Suppress	Minimize mixture diversity by removing it from your consciousness—by assigning it to the subconscious.
5. Isolate	Address diversity by including and setting "different" mixture components off to the side.
6. Tolerate	Address diversity by fostering a room-for-all attitude, albeit with limited superficial interactions among the mixture components.
7. Build relationships	Address diversity by fostering quality relationships—characterized by acceptance and understanding—among the mixture components.
8. Foster mutual adaptation	Address diversity by fostering mutual adaptation in which all components change somewhat, for the sake of achieving common objectives.

Option 1: Include/Exclude

This is the option that most people are familiar with, and it is the one that undergirds most affirmative action efforts, where the goal is primarily to increase the number of target-group members in the organization at all hierarchical levels. Indeed, this is what most people mean by diversity. The flip side of include is exclude. Here, the goal is to minimize diversity by keeping diverse elements out or by expelling them once they have been included.

An example that reflects this option is the selection criteria used to screen candidates for employment; how these criteria are specified has a great deal to do with the resulting diversity mix. If your firm needs engineers and you require a degree in electrical engineering, you are automatically limiting the diversity of expertise. Another example can be found in the ways corporations deal with their stockholders. Consider those companies that have tried to minimize stockholder participation in decision making; that's exclusion. On the other hand, the current response of companies to investors' demand for greater participation in decisions is an example of inclusion.

Option 2: Deny

In this option, everyone denies that differences exist. Historically, denial has played a major role in managerial thinking, particularly for managers who limit their understanding of diversity to workforce issues. They practice denial when they tell employees who are different that their differences will not in any way affect how the organization treats them, that merit and performance alone will determine how far they can go. People of different races, for instance, are told, with pride, that the organization is color blind.

Or consider the manager in a company that has been recently acquired who is introducing someone from the parent corporation to his staff and says the visitor is "not like the rest of those corporate guys." This person has earned the privilege of having his corporate status denied; he is receiving "corporate-blind" treatment.

Another example: the manager who looks at proposed options for change and says "nothing new here; we're already doing those things." This manager is denying any

difference between the status quo and the new proposals—
which of course makes it unnecessary to consider the change
in question.

Option 3: Assimilate

The basic premise of this option is that all elements that are
different, that are in the minority somehow, will learn to become like the dominant element. Minority employees will
learn to fit in; a new overseas operation will be structured just
like, and will run just like, the home office; new products will
be manufactured using the same processes as older products.

Assimilation has been the dominant approach to differences and diversity across all kinds of dimensions. It is especially prominent in organizations that have experienced
substantial economic success. In this case, assimilation makes
eminent sense. The companies have worked out their formulas for effectiveness and efficiency and see no need to change.
All can join as long as they adapt to proven ways of winning.

The difficulty arises, of course, when the tried and true
formulas no longer produce the same results. When your environment is becoming destabilized, it is foolish to blind
yourself to new ideas and to insist on continuing past practices through full assimilation.

An example of assimilation gone awry is seen in companies where one particular function dominates the organization. For example, in some companies the dominant function
is marketing. It's part of the culture; you often hear people
say, "We are a marketing company." The problem comes
when members of the dominant function insist that everyone
do business from its perspective. This immediately discounts
the contribution of people from other functions, transforms
them into second-class citizens, and leads to dysfunctional
situations like this one:

An executive in a long-established company decided to
implement cross-functional teams as a means of gaining competitive advantage. As representatives from Manufacturing,

Marketing, Sales, Research and Development, and Account-ing were appointed, division managers found that minorities and women were not excited about participating. They were convinced that white males would make all the decisions, that the status quo would continue. While the division man-agers professed surprise about these sentiments, they really were shocked that people from the *nondominant functions* also felt the same way, but for different reasons. Their view was that Manufacturing, the dominant function, would ultimately make decisions, so why go through this charade?

Here's another example of assimilation that doesn't work. A Fortune 100 firm started a new line of business to complement the dominant line. The new line grew beyond the most optimistic projections, but its managers complained loudly that they were being stifled by the managers of the dominant line, who insisted that all lines should operate in the same manner, even though their markets differed greatly. The arguing became so intense that eventually the firm's ex-ecutives agreed to allow the new line to operate as an inde-pendent subsidiary. In essence, as assimilation failed they turned to segregation. (This is the action option called "isola-tion," described below.)

There's another problem with assimilation as it relates to the workforce. Members of minority groups—be they groups delineated by race, gender, physical abilities, whatever—are increasingly disinclined to embrace assimilation. "Thank you very much," they are saying, "but I'm not all that interested in becoming like you. If you don't mind [and—unspoken—even if you do], I'm going to keep my differences." We will look more closely at this trend in Chapter 5.

Option 4: Suppress

In this option, entities with differences are encouraged to keep a lid on them, not to manifest them. Suppression (some-times used in conjunction with assimilation) differs from denial in that the differences are recognized and acknowledged, but greatly discouraged for the good of the enterprise.

Many people who exercise suppression sincerely believe that the organization is greater than any one individual or component and that, since the organization has been operating well with the status quo, entities with differences should submerge them for the sake of the enterprise.

At the end of a presentation on diversity not long ago, a senior executive—a white male—said to me, in tones reflecting anger and frustration, "I'm tired of all this whining and complaining. Why can't people today sacrifice like we did? All you hear today is 'I' or 'me.' What about the greater good? Can't we rise above this selfishness?"

Then there is the "you've got to pay your dues" sentiment. Listen to a senior white-female executive: "On one hand, I hear with empathy the needs of minorities and women. But on the other hand, I become angry. I paid my dues. I did what I had to. This is life in corporations. Grow up! In this context, I'm not sympathetic at all."

This "pay your dues" assumption also shows up in the way people relate to new employees who openly question the status quo. Old-timers respond smugly, "How long have you been here?" What they mean is "Suppress your questions until you've been here long enough to understand." They're also saying, "If you just try it, you'll like it." In other words, "If you give our way a chance, you'll discover how sensible and right we are."

All these assumptions are undermined by today's realities. In turbulent economic environments, the old ways are not always right, and joining a corporation is not like joining a fraternity, where membership depends on sacrificing and paying your dues. Rather, the primary concern is doing what is necessary to assure the viability of the enterprise. Any dues-paying or sacrificing will be dictated not by *internal* traditions but by what is happening in the environment that affects the organization's viability.

Option 5: Isolate

Isolation allows you to include people or other entities that are different from the dominant system without having to change corporate culture or systems; you simply set the "different" entity off to the side. For example:

• A large urban church, historically predominantly white, recently has seen large influxes of Hispanics. The members responded by recruiting a Hispanic minister and encouraging the Hispanics to worship at a Spanish-language service at 3 P.M. This is isolation. The rationale was that these people with a different culture and language could better be served by someone who speaks their language and understands their culture.

• Managers often isolate new ideas; they simply call them "pilot" projects. If the manager likes the idea, he pilots it in a corner where it can grow and thrive. If he isn't excited about the idea, he isolates it in a corner where it will not be well received and eventually die.

• A large corporation doing business in many countries has few professionals in its U.S. headquarters who are familiar with business circumstances abroad. Company executives elect to treat these operations as if they were subsidiaries and encourage the local managers to make their own decisions. Here, isolation of the foreign operations is seen as a practical necessity and will probably continue until headquarters broadens its managerial capability.

• Managers group similar tasks into functions, creating isolated and relatively independent entities commonly called "silos." Isolation here promotes an environment especially suited for the functional tasks at hand. The more extreme the isolation, the more pronounced the silo around the function and the thicker the walls.

Option 6: Tolerate

You may think of this as the live-and-let-live option. Here, managers allow the inclusion of entities with differences, but they do not value these entities or accept their differences. They simply acknowledge their right to exist.

For example: A major corporation bought a smaller, very successful, cutting-edge technology company and set it up as a subsidiary. The acquired company had in place a very nontraditional culture that contributed greatly to its success and was very different from that of the new parent. When asked about this new subsidiary, parent representatives would smile and shake their heads. "They're weird, but they're good at what they do. As long as they make money for us, we don't bother them. I just try to talk to them as little as possible." Managers from the parent company neither understood nor endorsed the subsidiary culture. They simply segregated and tolerated it, allowing different behavior as long as it proved effective. Tolerance is made easier by the extent to which direct interaction can be avoided.

The tolerate option is grounded in the assumption that for the sake of the broader good, diverse entities can coexist without understanding, endorsing, or engaging each other affectively. This is a critical distinction between isolation and toleration. Isolation artificially limits its target; toleration does not limit, but rather simply never emotionally connects. Where toleration is used, you see managers of a new business line who never have felt accepted, or a racially different family in the neighborhood who does not feel discriminated against but yet does not feel accepted and valued.

This "coexisting without connecting" assumption is indeed well founded in an institution with a stable environment. In the bureaucratic institution, entities can contribute to the broader picture without true engagement or with minimum interaction, since they follow well-defined roles that require little cross-communication or cross-learning.

Often toleration and inclusion are used together. With an

inclusion focus, the question is whether the entity is present or taken into account, not whether it is connected with emotionally. Organizations concerned primarily about inclusion can more easily accept the limited involvement associated with tolerance. Thus, you have people proudly making certain, in a mechanical way, that the target entity is included.

Presently, the toleration alternative is being compromised. Environments characterized by uncertainty are not compatible with toleration because they require that people collaborate more. Collaboration needs much more intensive engagement and interaction than normally is the case with toleration.

Collaboration is further hampered by this reality: The act of toleration essentially is a condescending behavior. In effect the tolerator is saying, "By my grace, I am moved to allow your inclusion and coexistence." This condescension highlights the power imbalance between the parties. The "different" entity is repeatedly reminded of its subordinate position, even as the tolerator is becoming more tolerant. Limited engagement further exacerbates the feeling of not being valued. With a portion of units or employees feeling weak and undervalued, a corporation that practices toleration is greatly handicapped when it must adapt to dynamic environments.

The tension associated with toleration is one of the significant driving forces behind the interest in the workplace initiatives generally known by the name *valuing differences.* (In the Diversity Paradigm, this is the option called building relationships.) The pain of not being valued while being tolerated produces a preoccupation with valuing differences. Indeed, when many managers talk of differences and diversity, they frequently speak of the need to value.

Option 7: Build Relationships

In this option, deliberate efforts are made to foster relationships between the various entities. The governing assumption is that a good relationship can overcome differences. While this approach has the potential to foster acceptance and understanding of differences, often it is used to *minimize* them. This happens when the governing assumption is interpreted as follows: "If we just can talk and learn more about each other, despite our differences, I think we'll find many similarities that can be grounds for a mutually beneficial relationship." In other words by focusing on *similarities*, the hope is to avoid challenges associated with differences.

A number of familiar activities flow from this type of reasoning. Efforts to improve race relations represent one example. The challenge in these situations is to foster acceptance and understanding among the races. Another illustration would be the rotation of key executives among the various functions, fostering cross-functional understanding and relationships. Most team-building sessions are efforts at building relationships; they aim to enhance problem solving, collaboration, and communication among the participants. Finally, sensitivity training targeted to help participants get in touch with their prejudices and stereotyping capabilities falls into the category of relationship building.

Option 8: Foster Mutual Adaptation

Under this alternative, the parties involved accept and understand differences and diversity, recognizing full well that doing so may call for adaptation by all concerned. That is, to fully accommodate the entire diversity mixture and all its components and to facilitate maximum contribution to organizational objectives, every entity—not just the ones that are different—will have to make some changes.

This option is just evolving as a concept. Only a few corporations have moved forward to set the stage for implementation. Just developing the appropriate mindset represents a major challenge for most companies. Most of them reflect an attitude illustrated by the following fable.

Suppose you and I have met at a seminar in New Mexico and I invite you to visit me in Atlanta. Some weeks later, you take me up on my offer. I say to you, "While you're here, make yourself at home. My house is your house." After a couple of days, we debrief. You express appreciation for my hospitality and the reception offered by my family. In fact, you'd like to stay two weeks. But you have a concern: You are a gourmet cook and my kitchen is not set up for gourmet cooking. Gently you explain that we will have to remodel the kitchen. My response is, "That's not what I had in mind when I said 'make yourself at home.' What I had in mind was that you would make yourself at home within the context of what exists. I did not envision major revisions."

The "foster mutual adaptation" alternative argues that remodeling the house may be necessary—not for the benefit of those who are different, but for the sake of the viability of the enterprise.

This attitude is often difficult for managers in organizations with a history of success. The last thing they wish to do is to disturb a successful status quo. But today's comfortable success is very likely to be threatened by tomorrow's unpredictable challenges, and they may be forced to do just that. Mutual adaptation permits the greatest accommodation of diversity, which means that it enhances ability to deal with overwhelming complexity. When your status quo starts to develop tiny fracture lines running in all directions, a mutual adaptation mindset may be your best weapon against disaster.

Understanding the Action Options

Five points regarding these action options merit our careful attention

1. *Of the eight options, only one unequivocally endorses diversity.* The other seven seek to minimize or eliminate diver-

sity and complexity. That one option is foster mutual adaptation, and it is so new, we are not yet very familiar with it. Can a society that traditionally has heavily used seven options for minimizing diversity make a turnaround and value diversity? Yes, but not quickly. We need to be aware of this reality so that we can establish realistic goals for change.

Incidentally, there are times when it is appropriate to limit diversity or to simplify complexity significantly. The point here is to realize that many managers will have difficulty perceiving and reacting to diversity that is dictated by situational parameters.

2. *None of the action options is inherently good or bad in itself: It all depends on the context.* I wish to emphasize this: All options are legitimate and can be used positively or negatively. Accepting this proposition is a challenge for people who have looked at diversity only in the framework of race and gender. Is it really true, for example, that the dreaded isolation (segregation) practices of the Old South and South Africa could ever be a positive? Let's sample a few possibilities.

Exclude: When you're trying to get work done, there is such a thing as too much diversity or inappropriate diversity. Once *true* requirements have been identified (as opposed to preferences, conveniences, or traditions), exclusion is a legitimate way to assemble a workforce congruent with the needs of the enterprise. This would be positive for the company and ultimately for the associates who did not "fit."

Deny: Denial can be an effective and appropriate coping mechanism until there is a state of *readiness* for diversity or differences. An example: A woman manager in a major corporation found herself struggling for three years to meld her unit into a team. Although some progress was

made, she reached a plateau with much left un-
done. One day a helpful friend commented, "I
sense that there are some real issues of racism
and sexism here." After reflection, the manager
said, "I guess so. Maybe I have been denying
this. I simply wasn't ready to deal with it." Now,
the manager is strategizing how to raise these issues in ways that will foster team building.

Readiness is a powerful notion. Action before
readiness is likely to be futile. In the meantime,
life must go on and progress must be made. A
caution here is that you must continuously test
your understanding of reality to avoid relying on
denial beyond the point of readiness. This is as
undesirable as acting too soon.

Isolate: The company that took a hands-off approach to
global operations until sufficient managerial capability could be developed at headquarters was
using isolation in a positive way. The white
church that set up special services for its Hispanic members was practicing isolation also;
whether this is good or bad depends on the context. If the minister were to say, "We feel a moral
responsibility to give these people an opportunity to worship, but we have little desire or need
to interact with them," that's negative isolation.
But if his attitude is "We know we will have to
change the 11:00 A.M. service eventually, but we
do not know how. By allowing the new members
to worship at 3:00 P.M., we are setting up a transi-
tional arrangement where their worship needs
can be met until we determine how to modify
the main service. In the meantime, the two
groups can visit each other in preparation for
identifying the parameters of the new unified
service," that's also isolation, but it's positive.

Assimilate: Assimilation is an essential for all organizations—no ifs, ands, or buts about it. This statement may be surprising given all I have said about people's new attitude toward assimilation. The reality, however, is that once a company's management has identified *true* requirements, it must move to foster conformity through assimilation. Unless this conformity is achieved, fulfillment of these requirements will be less than desired. The challenge is not with assimilation in and of itself, but rather the inappropriate use of it. When people are forced to assimilate over issues that are not important to key forces in the business environment, or over nonessentials like company traditions or personal preferences, that is inappropriate use. And that's when you will find people quietly, or perhaps even loudly, rebelling.

3. *Action choices can be used in combination.* They do not have to be used one at a time. Think, for instance, of corporate culture regarding new employees: people may be recruited (included) and isolated; recruited and merely tolerated; or recruited and asked to suppress and assimilate. Similarly, one company might buy (include) another company and then set it up as a subsidiary (isolation).

4. *The selection of action choices is dynamic and determined by context.* The next section of this chapter discusses the process of choosing options. The point here is that as your context changes, you might need to select another action. The appropriateness of any choice can vary with circumstance.

5. *Each option can be used with* any *collective mixture of differences and similarities.* While we are most familiar with them in the context of race and gender, they can be found where there is diversity of any kind.

Selecting a Course of Action

First, a word of caution is in order. People who are not yet comfortable with diversity in the full sense of the word can become very frustrated at this point. In working with the Diversity Paradigm they are faced with eight choices—a diversity mixture in itself, and a potentially overwhelming one. Catch-22. So before you dive into making your choice, make sure that you have done everything you can to increase your understanding of what diversity really is.

Then how do you go about selecting the appropriate option or blend of options? I believe it is a function of at least five factors: your point of reference, individual inclination, individual mindset, organizational environment, and diversity tension.

Point of Reference

The person dealing with the mixture in question has the option of seeing himself as a part of the set or as apart from it. This is not an academic distinction. Where you position yourself affects the nature of your actions. To take an obvious example, white males who define diversity mixtures as something that includes them see diversity differently from those who define diversity as external to themselves.

The basketball player wishing to enhance the performance of a diverse mixture called "the team" can approach the task from a perspective within the mixture or outside it. The manager addressing the morale of a diversity mixture called "the workforce" can see himself as a part of the group or as apart from the group. The CEO desiring to improve the effectiveness of her executive committee can see herself as a part of this mixture or as separate from it.

There is, of course, a third possibility: she sees herself as simultaneously a member of both sets—which is, of itself, a diversity mix.

Personal Inclination and Mindset

Your choice of action is also influenced by two related personal factors: your diversity inclination and your mindset. Inclinations, not unlike the tendency to be left-handed, are developed early in life, and can be difficult to change. Mindset, your way of thinking about an issue, is much more current than inclination. My inclination, based on early learnings, teachings and experiences, may be to not trust or respect white males, but my mindset is that *some* white males are worthy of trust and respect, given that some of my *current* best friends are white males.

Mindsets can reinforce inclinations or stifle them. The greater the incongruence, the greater the psychological stress you will experience. Similarly, people are not always able to act on their inclinations and mindsets. Here are some examples:

• My inclination and my mindset may be to avoid black males, but they represent a significant portion of my workforce; in fact some of my best employees are black males. If I refuse to relate to them, I will not be able to achieve my objectives. So I cannot act on my inclination or my mindset, which creates serious stress.

• My inclination and mindset may be to accept all individuals, regardless of their differences. However, because I am not skilled in changing systems or building cultures, I am unable to build an organization that reflects my inclination and mindset. A lack of managerial skills limits the ability to act on my inclination and mindset.

Organizational Environment

Environmental factors have forced managers to put diversity on their agenda, and environmental factors influence their responses to it. When the world you do business in is changing rapidly, then your environment is forcing you to change as well. Even if your personal inclination might pull you in one direction in regard to diversity, the external environment may be pulling even harder in another direction. Change *is* diversity; in a complex, turbulent environment the only constancy you will have is the constancy of change. You may have to surrender your personal inclinations.

For instance, you may prefer to see functions in the organization structured as independent units, working autonomously. But if external circumstances are forcing you to, say, develop new products much faster and get them quickly to market, you can no longer afford this separation. Or you might prefer to practice denial in relation to some workforce issue, but workers and peers might not allow that option.

Diversity Tension

In Chapter 1, I mentioned the critical question of tension, especially "bad" tension, in diagnosing the situation and deciding on a course of action. At a minimum you need to assess the nature of the diversity tensions, their intensity, and their impact on the bottom line.

If you note the presence of tension, and if it is interfering with maximum realization of what you consider the organization's key success factors, then you must ask yourself:

- Given our mission and success factors, what is the desired state with respect to the diversity tension?
- Which of the Paradigm's options have the greatest potential to bring about that desired state?

In sum, several factors interact to influence your selection of action options. Some of them are internal: your point of reference, inclination, and mindset. And some of them are external to you: the organizational environment and the nature and intensity of any diversity tension.

Depending on the circumstances, any one of these factors, or any combination, can be dominant at any particular time. This can be a hard lesson for highly motivated managers: No matter what your personal inclination and mindset toward these issues, sometimes external factors can block certain options from consideration. But regardless of your mindset, you *will* face diversity, and you *will* be affected by it.

3

Revitalizing Dinosaurs

There are cities and companies, unions and political parties
that are like dinosaurs waiting for the weather to change.
The weather is not going to change. The very ground is
shifting beneath us. And what is called for is nothing less
than all of us reconceptualizing our roles.

—John Naisbitt, *Megatrends*

In recent years we have witnessed a phenomenon most ob-
servers would previously have thought impossible: the stum-
bling, fumbling, and even near-total collapse of some of our
largest business organizations. Corporations that have been
eminently successful in the past, that have dominated their
industries for decades, now find themselves in serious difficulty. Many are struggling to maintain their competitive
superiority; some are literally fighting to survive. The possibility that these previously dominant organizations may become dinosaurs is real.[1]

Because these potential dinosaurs are large corporations,
size is often cited as the culprit. It is possible, however, that
the significant causal factor is not bigness but the *institutionalized* nature that often characterizes most of these dinosaur
candidates.

The Evolution of Dinosaurs

How did this happen? How did these giant companies reach
such a precarious position, and what can be done about it? Re-

garding the first question, I believe that the evolutionary process toward dinosaurism is reasonably predictable. If we look at business organizations from the historian's perspective, we can see that they all progress through the same four developmental phases: Exploration, Eureka, Institutional, and Survival (see Exhibit 3-1). The fourth phase is the watershed; at this point, companies either cycle back through earlier behaviors, or try something new. That "something new" is, in terms of this evolutionary process, Phase 5: the business phase.[2] And those companies smart enough to move into this phase provide us with the answer to the second question: What can be done?

At each phase in the evolution, leaders and managers of organizations demonstrate some of the traits associated with the various options of the Diversity Paradigm. They probably do not recognize that is what they are doing, but we do, and this recognition helps us analyze what is occurring.

Phase 1: Exploration

In the initial, or Exploration, phase the founder begins with a business idea he/she believes in. Then, either formally or

Exhibit 3-1. The phases of organizational development.

Phase	Dominant Responses to Diversity Mixtures
1. Exploration (searching for the success formula)	Inclusion, building relationships, mutual adaptation
2. Eureka (exploiting and celebrating the success formula)	Exclusion, assimilation
3. Institutional (perfecting the success formula)	Exclusion, assimilation, suppression, segregation, denial, toleration
4. Survival (fighting fires)	Inclusion, toleration
5. Business (adapting continuously to the changing external environment)	Inclusion, building relationships, mutual adaptation

informally or both, he/she analyzes him/herself and the existing business environment. These analyses give rise to basic, fundamental assumptions about requirements for business success and form the basis of the company's original culture.

The founder then launches practices that are congruent with those assumptions. The ones that work are retained; the ones that don't are discarded. This process is repeated many times, until assumptions and practices are in place to assure the corporation's success. In other words, the founder continues the search until he/she discovers the formulas for success.

During this Exploration phase, the founder desires specific attributes from associates: commitment to the organization, openness to new ideas, comfort with the learning mode, and tolerance for risk, ambiguity, and disappointment.

People in the new company demonstrate an easy acceptance of diversity. In their search for success formulas, they willingly embrace all people and practices that might help in the search, even ones that are "different." They are, in effect, using three tools from the Diversity Paradigm: inclusion, building relationships, and mutual adaptation. Learning and problem solving are priority considerations.

Phase 2: Eureka

Once the success formulas are discovered, the founder moves to fully exploit them. In the Eureka phase, the emphasis is on growing the company and keeping up with expanding demand for its products or services. This is a heady time, a time of excitement and success. Those who hung in during the Exploration phase now begin to reap their just rewards. Those who join at this point have an opportunity to jump on a train as it leaves the station for what promises to be a fruitful experience.

This is also the first glimpse of a critical diversity issue: those who were here for the founding versus those who came later. Special benefits accrue to those who were around during the founding era, and this can produce a particularly divisive form of diversity tension. Also in this period, the initial organizational assumptions, refined during the Exploration phase, are being reaffirmed and are beginning to take root. The company's culture and character are emerging, and employees are taking pride in their evolving enterprise.

Associates are expected to demonstrate respect for the founder, loyalty to the company and its success formulas, an openness to taking directions (for those joining at this stage), and a comfort with rigidity. Given the dynamic character of companies at this stage, this last quality may seem surprising. Yet even though the organization is young and its culture is emerging, rigidity with respect to practices sets in very quickly.

The sources of this rigidity are the magnitude of the success and the short period of time in which it occurred. People with new ideas are often met with this sentiment: "If you're so smart, why didn't *you* found the company? Since you didn't and since the founder's ideas are working, shut up and fall in line—or get out!" The diversity tension between founding and nonfounding associates often reaches significant levels in this stage, and is joined by other tensions as well: between critical and noncritical players and between insiders (those part of the company) and outsiders (those part of the external environment).

Exclusion and assimilation tend to be the dominant tools for addressing diversity and complexity at this stage. Participants now believe that life is not complex after all, that their newfound formulas clarify all mysteries. Only true believers are welcome. Those who are not true believers at recruiting are expected to become so through assimilation after joining. Acceptance of diversity is on the decline. Indeed, at this point the climate is often comparable to that of a religious cult.

What happens after the Eureka stage? It depends on its duration. If the phase is short-lived, managers will return to the Exploration phase to further refine the success formulas. But if the second phase lasts for a significant period or if it catapults the corporation to a leadership role in its industry, managers move to institutionalize the success formulas. They would be foolish not to.

Phase 3: Institutional

Here, managers take steps to ensure that deviation from the success formulas is minimized. They are convinced that their formulas, having passed the tests of the marketplace with flying colors, will remain valid for the foreseeable future. It then becomes logical to use bureaucracy to lock in the desired behavior by minimizing discretionary decision making and the possibility of deviation that would inevitably accompany it.

Bureaucracy brings with it a heavy emphasis on control to ensure appropriate behavior. There is no need for learning or experimentation; in fact, those traits are no longer valued. Employees are expected to be hardworking, to emphasize doing more than thinking, to follow the established success formulas and take directions unquestioningly, to work within narrowly defined specialized roles, and to be comfortable receiving a restricted flow of information limited to just their specific roles. These expectations give rise to a very stable corporate culture. Root assumptions and practices are firmly embedded, and the stage is set for perpetual success.

Many American corporations have been in this phase for a very long time, so long that their leaders take competitive advantage and market success as givens. The longer this success continues, the more institutionalized the organization becomes.

Managers of institutions do not welcome diversity. They respond to it with exclusion, denial, segregation, suppression, assimilation, and toleration. The very idea of making changes to the success formula is heresy, and thus managers staunchly resist evidence of any environmental changes that would require internal modifications.

But the changes are happening anyway, with such an intensity that they cannot be denied. Now, many companies are finding that the very strengths that once made them the leaders in their industries are actually serious weaknesses in the midst of substantial environment change.[3]

Navigating "permanent white water." Make no mistake about it: the business environment *is* changing, and from several directions at once. Powerful changes are occurring in the external environment your organization does business in, and also in the dynamics of important groups of stakeholders. Collectively, these changes mean that your earlier success formulas are becoming obsolete—if they aren't already.

The current external business environment is often described as "permanent white water," and it is a very apt description.[4] Many managers see their situation as like the continuous chaos of a wild river, with one difficult set of rapids after another and no recovery time in between.

A basic premise of this book is that the turbulence of today's corporate environment is a manifestation of diversity and complexity. Managers unable to accept the diversity of their environment simply cannot take steps to adapt as necessary. Even when they are able to recognize and accept the reality of diversity, some managers simply cannot process it cognitively and emotionally. The magnitude of changes pushes against their cognitive and emotional limits. They desperately want to believe that calm waters are ahead and if they can get through this one last rough spot, they won't have to make any permanent changes. My sense is that *all* the water downstream is white and will remain so for the foreseeable future. I think few—if any—managers and their corporations can survive the costs of not changing.

In addition to the chaos of general business conditions, corporations are faced with changes in the makeup of three important groups: employees, customers, and stockholders. The reality of shifting demographics is causing enormous changes in the workforce[5] and in the consumer population,[6] changes that are well documented elsewhere. Stockholder dynamics are changing as well. The rise of so-called relationship investing, in which investors buy and hold sizable blocks of stock and monitor management's performance, means that executives can no longer ignore stockholders.[7] All these various groups have different expectations.

What makes it difficult and complex for managers is that they have not had to consider these entities in the past—at least not simultaneously. So senior managers accustomed to juggling one environmental ball at a time are now required to keep at least three or four in the air—all the while navigating a river full of treacherous rapids.

In such a world, relying on formulaic procedures makes little sense. Institutionalization and bureaucracy make excellent sense if a company has the success formula *and* a stable environment. But once the environment becomes unstable, all bets are off. The company's executives then must move to make serious adjustments or risk becoming prisoners of their successful past.

A common reaction is to assume that the environmental changes have caused a major, but *temporary,* incongruence between organizational practices and external realities. The leaders vow to pull all the stops to ensure survival until normalcy returns. They move to Phase 4.

Phase 4: Survival

The Survival phase focuses on efficiency, on doing more with less in order to ride out the crisis. A strong emphasis is placed on downsizing or rightsizing: adjusting the scale of operations downward while maintaining or raising expectations with respect to output. Sometimes this is described as "back to basics," back to what made the corporation great initially.

With the urgency associated with crisis, managers here attach a premium to reacting to and putting out fires. They pay more attention to the external environment and free up information flow to facilitate fire fighting. They also may reach out to remedies such as total quality, reengineering, and the learning company. Unfortunately, the short-term focus of the Survival phase does not foster the in-depth change that these remedies require, so implementation lags greatly behind the enthusiasm of the moment.

Managers in the Survival phase often experience significant diversity and complexity in the form of new organizational practices and executives from the outside. They react with toleration: They embrace the outsiders and the new practices because of the crisis, but they do not connect with them emotionally. So when the frenzy of activity produces improvements and the crisis subsides, the institutional managers gleefully announce, "See, things were not really that bad. There's a lot of good about how we used to do business." They then start pushing for a return to the proven formulas, for things to get "back to normal."

Phase 5: Business

This urge to return to the Institutional phase is understandable, especially for those managers who know nothing else, but it is dangerous. The Institutional phase, remember, works only when your environment is stable, and the consensus is growing that we will not see stability for a long time to come.

The more farsighted organizations will instead move to the Business phase, which involves a continuous adaptation search for new success formulas. It is in all likelihood far more complex and difficult than the original search in the Exploration phase, simply because the business world is changing so profoundly that the search must go against the grain of institutionalized practices.

Moving to the Business framework, where change can be deep, calls for major shifts in managerial roles and mindsets. Cultural shifts are necessary too. A company in the Business phase values:

- Commitment to a shared mission and vision, as context for the reformulation
- Effectiveness—a focus on determining the right thing

to do, as opposed to determining how to do the right thing with the least resources

- Reflection and a learning capability
- Empowerment (in the search for something new, informed self-direction is necessary)
- Multifunctional roles with collaboration across units
- Management of performance, not just potential
- Strategic thinking*—the process of identifying approaches for gaining a sustainable competitive advantage in the future
- Cultural renewal—a sustained change in root assumptions
- Continuous searching and learning

Managers operating in the Business phase are using three Diversity Paradigm options: inclusion, building relationships, and mutual adaptation. They are open to outsiders and new practices. The expectation is that outsiders and the original corporate managers will collaborate in understanding each other's perspectives and in developing new strategic parameters. These managers see few black-and-white situations but understand that innovative combinations will be needed. They are also willing to experiment for the purpose of learning.

Moving into the Business phase requires acceptance and understanding of diversity. The learning, empowerment, tolerance for ambiguity/uncertainty, and major change implicit in this phase are all facilitated by a capability to address diversity effectively.

Diversity Management in the Business Phase

As managers of organizations seek to keep their enterprises appropriately aligned with environmental realities, they

*This ability has grown rusty in many companies that spent a long time in the Institutional phase.

must come to grips with four diversity mixtures that have a critical impact on their success: external realities, opportunities for learning, time perspectives, and processes for managing change. This reality provides us with a powerful example of a principal thesis of this book: Diversity in its broadest sense applies not merely to a collection of people who are alike in some ways and different in others, but also to intangibles—ideas, procedures, ways of looking at things. It also demonstrates the flexibility and usefulness of the Diversity Paradigm as a tool for making decisions when faced with a mixture of diverse elements.

Environmental Perceptions

On an ongoing basis, managers formally and informally receive impressions—snapshots, if you will—from their external environments. Collectively these snapshots constitute a picture of the current environment and serve as a framework for determining strategy and action plans.

For discussion purposes let's presume that at any given time a manager relies on his last ten snapshots as the operative portrait of external realities. In a stable environment, this mix of snapshots is relatively homogeneous; each photo is substantially similar to all the others. The manager can reasonably conclude that the external environment remains unchanged and he can continue business as usual.

But as the environment becomes more fluid, the resultant mix of ten snapshots is significantly diverse. Any one snapshot shows a scene quite different from the other nine, and furthermore the cumulative portrait is quite different from the view displayed by the earlier group of ten. The more unpredictable and dynamic the environment, the more diverse his collection of current snapshots *and* the more they vary in the aggregate from previous sets of ten. This manager is now looking at evidence of tension between the reality of today and the familiar status quo of yesterday. The key questions raised by this tension are, "Do I need to change my understanding of external reality? If so, will a change in the way we do business be required?"

To answer these questions, he must first decide what to do with respect to the diversity of the snapshots. His options include at least the following:

Exclude (avoid):	By choosing this option, the manager refuses to consider any snapshots that deviate significantly from the status quo, thereby ensuring that whatever shots are included will resemble the status quo.
Include:	Elects to include all snapshots, whether or not they resemble the status quo.
Deny:	Includes perceptions that are different but minimizes the differences. Typical comments are: "I don't see how this differs from what we've seen before"; "The more things change, the more they remain the same."
Isolate:	Includes snapshots that are different but sets them apart in a kind of holding pen. The manager is aware of them on a day-to-day basis, but as isolated entities that should not yet be used as grounds for action.
Suppress:	Places snapshots that differ too much from the status quo out of his day-to-day awareness. An inability to explain or understand the differences can serve as a rationale for suppression.
Assimilate:	Implicitly or explicitly interprets all current snapshots as part of the

	status quo, allowing him to state that the environment remains unchanged: "This is the same scene from a different angle"; "You look at this closely and you will recognize it from past snapshots."
Tolerate:	Includes snapshots that are different but does not give them enough significant weight to cause change in his composite view of the environment: "These new snapshots do not invalidate our previous portrait of external realities; they simply expand it. The two different portraits can coexist."
Build relationships:	Decides to test the different snapshots to determine how different they really are from the status quo: "The more we learn about these apparently different snapshots, the more alike they may actually be."
Foster mutual adaptation:	Accepts the reality that different snapshots will require adjusting his composite view of the environment.

All options are legitimate; the choice is determined by the reality of the environment. How the manager chooses to deal with this diversity mixture of environmental snapshots is critical, because if he loses touch with environmental realities, he will take inappropriate actions.

The Learning Process

The same analysis can be made with respect to the learning process. Learning requires a willingness and an ability to explore new experiences for the purpose of gleaning lessons and modifying your operating framework of knowledge. This framework influences your thinking and actions.

In this context, would-be learners must simultaneously address a mixture of accumulated learnings (the existing framework of knowledge) and opportunities offering the potential for new learnings. The more open you are and the more diversity you can handle, the greater your potential for learning. The task is to respond to learning opportunities in ways that are congruent with the business realities of your organization. Let's look at the learning process through the Paradigm's action choices.

Include: The person using this option actively seeks opportunities to learn and manifests a "continuous learning" attitude; welcomes diversity as a source of new lessons.

Exclude (avoid): Does not consider learning necessary or desirable, and so avoids any opportunity that might offer learning.

Deny: Is open to experiencing new opportunities, but then disallows their relevancy or significance.

Isolate: Goes through the experiences but sets the lessons gleaned apart as a special set of accumulated "inactive" knowledge, perhaps because of a perception that the organizational environment is not yet ready for the new learnings. Is aware of this learning, but does not consider it part of the active framework influencing action.

Suppress: Goes through the educational experiences, gleans lessons, and then suppresses them, from either a lack of understanding or a sense that the circumstances are not right to move forward. People who do not feel empowered frequently suppress to avoid the discomfort of disappointment.

Assimilate: Retains only the lessons that "fit" the existing accumulated knowledge; little change in behavior is likely.

Tolerate: Includes lessons in the governing body of knowledge but consciously ignores them; there is no significant change in thinking or action. This person is able to converse on the topic in an informed manner without making a full commitment to something he believes is only a fad.

Build relationships: Once this person notes that the concept appears not to be a fad and should be taken seriously, he moves to gain greater understanding of the lessons he has included in his framework. In particular, he is interested in contrasting the new part of the framework with the old, to determine how his thinking and actions might have to change. Eagerness for discussion and debate sometimes substitutes for changes in thinking and actions.

Foster mutual adaptation: Takes his existing framework of knowledge and combines it with new lessons into a new framework that gives rise to changes in thinking and action. Mutual adaptation is the process that produces individual Paradigm shifts.

Perspectives of Time

The third critical diversity mixture that must be dealt with effectively, if dinosaurism is to be avoided, is the mix of time perspectives—simultaneously coping with today's demands and tomorrow's opportunities. For some, this represents an enormous challenge. I believe it can be helpful to review that challenge through the action options of the Paradigm.

Exclude (avoid):	By necessity, most people have in their mixture the demands of the day, but many elect, for varying reasons, to consciously avoid the potentials of the future, thereby putting their organizations in great danger of entering tomorrow out of sync with environmental realities.
Include:	Elects to see the demands of the day and the potentials of the future as legitimate agenda items. The task becomes that of deciding how to address this mixture of current and future issues.
Deny:	Uses this option to include future opportunities but disallows the need to think in multiple time dimensions. Rationalizes with such comments as "Today's successes will be the building blocks for the future" (assuming that present and future will be similar), and "I'm taking one day at a time" (when the future seems uncertain). Denial of

Isolate: the need to think in the future tense is poor preparation for the future.

Includes and operationally embraces both present and future perspectives, but sets the future apart as "special." This person isolates futuristic thinking. This arrangement can foster a clearer understanding of the future, since thinking is not inhibited by present considerations, but can also limit transition planning. "We'll deal with the future when we get there."

Suppress: Accepts the need to think in the future tense but suppresses it to deal with today's pressures. When influenced by external forces— prompting or requests by others —this individual can relate well to the need to think about the future and can perhaps contribute significantly, but then reverts to suppression.

Assimilate: Thinks about the future only as an extrapolation of the present. In the context of turbulent environments, this is a dangerous assumption.

Tolerate: Accepts the need to think in terms of the future, but only as a necessary evil.

Build relationships: Strives to understand the differences and similarities between the present and the future. Clearly, this option goes further toward thinking in the present *and* future tenses. But there is a caution. If the future and the present are very different, thinking of the future in terms of the present can inhibit the ability to grasp the future. In addition, developing an understanding of the present and the future can become an end in itself, and thus not lead to strategic thinking and action.

Foster mutual adaptation: Is comfortable and skilled in moving back and forth between present realities and future potentials, and can do so as dictated by environmental realities. Has a clear understanding that the future must be understood on its own terms, and not solely in relationship to the present. This time perspective uniquely and operationally encompasses the present and future and enables effective behavior regarding present realities and future potentials.

Managing Change

Companies hoping to avoid dinosaurism not only must be able to accurately read environmental shifts, to function as a learning organization, and to develop a perspective of time that allows consideration of present and future issues, but must also have the capability to manage change.

If they are to successfully identify the nature of the desired change, change agents must come to grips early on with a diversity mixture of the status quo and its alternatives. The Diversity Paradigm can help them sort through this mixture.

Include: This change agent makes the conscious decision to consider the possibility of change, to create diversity mixtures of the status quo and alternatives.

Exclude (avoid):   Makes the conscious decision *not* to consider the possibility of change. A common rationale is "Things are OK. If it ain't broke, don't fix it."

Deny: Includes alternatives, but then disallows claims of differences that would make them worth considering. "Can you produce quantitative proof of results? If not, I cannot give it any credence." Or "Who else has adopted this approach? If no one else is doing it, it must not be worthwhile."

Isolate: Includes and embraces change alternatives but sets them apart as "special"; for example, puts total quality in place but considers it separate, a complement to the rest of the organization. The status quo is rarely affected.

Suppress: Considers and perhaps even favorably receives options but subsequently deliberately ignores them. May minimize change options by labeling them fads or by insisting they "will never fly in our culture."

Assimilate: Chooses to consider those options that either fit the status quo or can be redefined to fit, as in "We will develop our own version of succession planning." Appropriates the jargon of change while avoiding any real consideration of substantive change.

Tolerate: Includes the option as an alterna-

	tive but never really considers it seriously. A statement like "We're looking at strategic planning" never gets beyond its initial pronouncement.
Build relationships:	Consciously explores the options in the context of the status quo, expending considerable effort on understanding all aspects. If prolonged, this becomes the perpetual search for synergy.
Foster mutual adaptation:	Develops a new status quo, the result of a blending of the alternatives with the status quo to come up with a new desired state.

What we are talking about in this chapter is avoiding dinosaurism. The real dinosaurs from eons ago had no way of recognizing that the world around them was changing. These fascinating creatures, including many with enormous bodies and relatively tiny brains, spent their last days blissfully lumbering over the landscape, nibbling treetops and grasses alike or nibbling each other, completely unaware that their species were doomed to extinction.

American corporations can avoid that fate. They are large and sometimes clumsy, but they have the innate capacity to look over the horizon and analyze what they see, and to change course in response. Sometimes that capacity needs to be charged up, for it is true that the skill of strategic thinking has become rusty in some of our largest organizations, but the terror of trying to survive the crisis provides all the adrenaline most of them need.

To all who have their eyes open, the turbulent environment provides the motivation for change. Then to act clearly and decisively in the face of that motivation, these leaders need a way to analyze their options and make the choice that best advances their company's competitive position. To help with this process, the Diversity Paradigm is offered as a two-way tool. Managers who become facile with this tool are better at recognizing the diversity and complexity implicit in environmental changes, and better at effectively adapting to those changes. Managers with these skills can give their corporations profound strategic advantage.

4

The Leadership Challenge

In the business world today, few topics are discussed so freely, so frequently, or so passionately as the practice of management. Whether in praise or criticism, people often talk as if it is crystal clear what the proper role of management is. Yet conversations with managers indicate that they themselves are not clear. Indeed, it is not uncommon to find situations where "managers" refuse to use the word *managing* because of undesirable connotations.

Despite this confusion or because of it, prescriptions abound. Every day we hear calls for more empowerment, visioning, strategic thinking, culture change, and effective facilitation of work; yet relatively little progress has been made on these fronts. There are probably more books, studies, and consultant reports on management and leadership theories and skills than all other business-related materials combined; yet companies large and small are imploding for lack of real leadership and effective management.

Why Not More Progress?

With all the tools at our disposal, why haven't we made more progress? One possible answer is limited ability to handle the complexity of large-scale change, a situation exacerbated by the very complexity of the manager's day-to-day job responsibilities. So part of what we must do is to help managers find ways to become comfortable with complexity.

Another possible reason for unsustainable progress is

that in many organizations senior management pays only minor attention to what the rank-and-file middle managers do and how well they do it. When this happens, it can usually be traced to the widespread confusion about what "managing" entails. Senior managers think what they do is managing and what the lower-level managers do is something else, usually something less significant. In these companies, areas that represent legitimate managerial concerns, such as strategic planning, are reserved for senior managers, with the net effect that cohesiveness is lost and sources of good ideas are ignored. So another part of what we must do is redefine our understanding of the managerial role.

This is not an academic exercise; the need to redefine management is real and urgent. And it is most assuredly not simple. If it were easy, many companies would not be in the trouble they are in. It is even more difficult because it has to be done against a backdrop of chaos. Asking managers to think conceptually about what they are doing while they are preoccupied with doing it is like asking someone to pat his head and rub his stomach at the same time and to do so while jumping through an obstacle course of burning circles while the stopwatch is running.

What we need to do, I believe, is take the concept of management apart, examine its pieces, and put it back together again. In that undertaking, I believe the Diversity Management process, and the Diversity Paradigm, can bring some clarity to our thinking.

The Managerial Process

Everything that occurs in an organization, for good or bad, is enacted through people. What people in the company do, day to day and year to year, will determine success or failure. What they do is to some extent set by their managers (specific assignments) and to a larger but more subtle extent by their leaders (overall direction, vision, and culture).

As we set out to examine what management really means, let's begin with the notion that the manager and the leader might be the same person. The components of leading are not the same as the components of managing, but all managers are, I believe, both leader and manager. Everyone who has responsibility for the work of someone else fills both roles, in proportions that vary with the specific individuals and the situation at hand.

Also, the "managing" component of that dual role is itself composed of two components. Sometimes managers do the work of their department; sometimes they create the conditions that enable others to do the work. (Later in this chapter these will be described as the "doer framework" and the "empowerment framework.") These two complementary functions, like the duality of manager and leader, shift in relative proportion according to the dynamics at the time.

By now you can quickly recognize that these managers are faced with two simultaneous diversity mixtures: between doing and empowering, and between managing and leading. That's diversity squared: a mixture of mixtures. And that is the common condition of managerial life in most business organizations today. It's no wonder managers are burned out, leaders are stymied, and workers are distrustful.

Yet the fact that this dilemma can be viewed as a diversity problem also provides us a way to search for solutions. The Diversity Management process is a valuable tool in that search.

The Management Component

The management component of the managerial process essentially is the function of assuring that the company attains its short-term objectives. The job of the manager is to make certain that people do what is necessary to achieve short-term objectives. Toward that end, managers can function with two major frameworks: doer and empowerment.

The Doer Framework

The *doer framework* calls for the manager to do the business work and to take care of the employees, typically in the way a parent would take care of a child. So the marketing manager sees herself as doing marketing, as being the chief marketer, and also as providing the care necessary to ensure that employees are willing to assist as needed in pursuit of short-term organizational objectives. She perceives managerial tools as vehicles for providing that care. She views employees as extensions of herself.[1]

In theory, doer managers spend 50 percent of their time doing the work and the remaining 50 percent taking care of employees. However, in practice, if there is a crisis or a threat of one, managers spend the bulk of their time on doing the work. Under these crisis circumstances, the manager does not see herself as ignoring people, but rather as doing what she must as chief marketer to ensure that the business remains healthy and that employees remain employed.

Doer managers see themselves as having been promoted to manager because of their ability to do. Unless told otherwise, they assume that they are to continue as doers, with their employees as enablers or extensions that will allow them (the managers) to do more and to be of greater service to the organization. Their understanding is that they are not to become bogged down with human resources issues, but rather to refer them to the human resources department when they must. The doer manager looks to the human resources department for leadership and guidance in taking care of people issues. Ideally, the doer manager wishes to be able to take employee compliance as a given.

Explicit in the doer framework is the duality of business issues and people issues. Doer managers who focus primarily on business issues tend to be known as "task-oriented," while those viewed as addressing people issues are seen as "people managers" and as "sensitive and nice to have as a boss." Typically, corporations value the task-oriented, hands-on manager more than the people-oriented practitioner. While conducting research in organizations, I have often sensed that a social worker role has been assigned to the people-oriented managers and the human resources department.

In this doer setting, "managing" is often defined as dealing with people and is not valued. Not surprisingly, experienced managers often operate under the "inverse-pyramid assumption," which assumes that 80 percent of the people do 20 percent of the work and that 20 percent of the employees (the cream) do 80 percent of the work. Under this assumption, logic dictates minimum attention to "people issues."

How does the doer framework relate to Diversity Management? As you might expect, doer managers do not seek or desire diversity. They tend to see themselves as the principal doer and employees as extensions of themselves, their extra sets of hands. They expect employees upon signal to clone their behavior, and they have low tolerance for deviant behavior patterns. Furthermore, as you also might predict, doer managers frequently have as much difficulty with the M in Diversity Management as they do with the D. This is understandable. If you think *managing* means being nice to people—a behavior that doer managers devalue because it doesn't help get the work done—embracing managing as your primary activity requires an enormous mindset shift.

The Empowerment Framework

The *empowerment framework* differs from the doer mode in several ways. As a starting point, it does not assume the "inverse pyramid assumption." Rather it insists that the 80 percent must be enabled to contribute to their full potential in pursuit of short-term objectives. Empowerment managers see management tools as a way to facilitate that enabling process. They perceive a partnership, rather than a parental, arrangement between themselves and their subordinates. Schematically, the definition of empowerment[2] looks something like this:

Manager----▸ Management----▸ People ----▸ Desired ----▸Business
                    tools   behavior   objectives
                                                                  patterns

Empowerment is an example of terminology that is used without full understanding or full agreement as to meaning. I have observed that managers often talk of empowerment as if it were synonymous with hands-off, high-delegation management, which flies in the face of the continuing and growing popularity of hands-on management. I believe that hands-on involvement is very much congruent with empowerment. This involvement makes the manager's expertise, knowledge, experience, and common sense available to subordinates without fostering dependence, but by enhancing their capability and motivation.[3]

There also exists some concern about empowerment in relation to self-managing teams. I have heard managers talk as if self-managing teams make managing unnecessary, or if it is necessary, it is something that can be done by any empowered team member. According to this way of thinking, no special preparation is needed for managing; common sense is the only essential requirement. My own experiences show something different. As I have observed self-managing teams in corporations and academia, I have noted that as they mature a begrudging acknowledgement emerges that more than amateur management will be required, and that they need managerial support. As groups evolve, it is not uncommon to see training and education about the managerial role offered and accepted. Further, team members come to understand that managerial assistance is needed to complement and leverage their team efforts.

The Difference Between Doing and Empowering

Perhaps the best way to fully understand what empowerment means is to study how it differs from the doer framework.

The empowerment manager does not seek mere compliance, but rather engagement and commitment of the employees' total potential. Accordingly, desired behavior patterns are different under the two frameworks. The doer manager prescribes in detail the task-related behavior desired of employees; the empowerment manager solicits commitment and process behavior from employees that will enable them to play a major role in determining what task-related behavior should be. This desire for commitment is stimulated by challenges of turbulent environments and, in the words of one manager, the necessity for all players to be fully engaged in the game.

Also, the empowerment manager does not face the duality of business and people issues. If she is working on business issues, by definition she is working on people issues; if she is working on people issues, by definition she is working on business issues—since she is empowering employees toward attainment of short-term business objectives.

A related distinction is that if business objectives are achieved, the empowerment manager cannot say that she accomplished them, but rather that she *facilitated* the success. Indeed, the empowerment marketing manager cannot even describe herself as a marketer, but rather as a manager of marketers. Herein lies a major barrier to the transition from the doer model to the empowerment framework.

When a doer manager who is valued by herself and others as a marketer is asked to practice empowerment, she essentially is being asked to assume responsibilities not valued by her or her peers. She is being asked to take on illegitimate work—managerial work in the sense of empowering and enabling employees. Unless the manager believes in the rationale for empowerment management, she will revert back to the doer mode.

Obviously, this *facilitating empowerment* differs from the doer mode, where the manager essentially sees subordinates as clones of herself, micromanages their activities, and allows very little discretion. *Facilitating empowerment* gives subordinates discretion, requires effective rather than clone behavior, but yet also provides partnership assistance and involvement.

Doer/Empowerment Balance

Every manager's job has some D and some E component. The question is, what is the proper balance? How big should a given manager's D be with respect to her E? Generally speaking, the proportions are a function of the manager's place in the hierarchy. The higher you are, the larger your E should be in comparison to D; the lower you are on the ladder, the more pronounced your D becomes (see Exhibit 4-1). I believe this is especially true in the midst of a white-water environment. Also, striking the proper balance between D and E is a dynamic process; managers must be ready to shift their relative reliance on one approach or the other, as circumstances dictate.

Changing Mindsets

No doubt you have inferred that I believe managers who have a doer orientation need to move toward the empowerment

Exhibit 4-1. The doer/empowerment mix in the corporate pyramid.

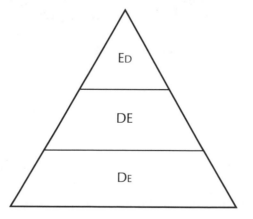

mode. This often involves a mindset shift of considerable proportions—important but not easy. To facilitate that shift, managers must address at a minimum the four diversity mixtures described in Chapter 3: environmental perceptions, learning, time perspectives, and change.

Accurately perceiving the environment is key. Without this accuracy, managers will remain unconvinced that moving toward empowerment has any connection to the bottom line. They may perceive it in terms of social and humanistic motives focused on doing something that will benefit individuals, but they perceive no business rationale. In the absence of a business rationale, they are unlikely to have sufficient motivation to work through the complexity that is involved in embracing empowerment.

Learning also will be crucial. Managers will have to learn new mindsets and skills. One central skill will be the contingency approach, using different mixtures of D and E at different hierarchical levels. This may be too complex for some managers. My experience in discussing the managerial role with managers has been that contingency prescriptions are not greeted warmly. They frequently see "it depends" as a cop-out response and seek in vain for the one right way. They also complain that too-frequent adjustments would be difficult to implement and, in moments of candor, admit doubt as to whether managers have the necessary adaptability. In essence, for some the contingency approach may be too complex to be practical.

One other skill will entail empowering without being hands-off and being involved without micromanaging. Doer managers will be tempted to translate *facilitating empowerment* as doer managing, which in the context of empowerment becomes micromanaging.

Learning will also have to occur around the conceptual diversity mixture of doer and empowerment management modes. Managers must be able to create such a mixture and secure the conceptual clarity required for implementation. Not only must managers be able to differentiate between doer

and empowerment management, but also between microma-
nagement and facilitating empowerment. All of this conceptual clarity is essential for striking the right doer/
empowerment balance.

The time-perspective diversity mixture has to be addressed. Because empowerment is a process that occurs over
time, more than a short-term framework will be required.
Managers who cannot operate within short-, mid-, and long-
term time frameworks will have difficulty moving toward
empowerment.

Finally, diversity mixtures with respect to change will
have to be considered. Often, I have found that managers
tend to minimize efforts at changing organizational parameters like culture, values systems, and processes; instead, their
notion of major change is massive training. Moving toward
empowerment and the appropriate D/E balance, however,
will call for changes in individual mindsets, attitudes, predispositions, skills, and behavior, *and* also modifications in organizational culture, values, systems, and processes. Without
change along both dimensions, progress will be difficult to
sustain.

Applying the Diversity Paradigm

In addition to those four mixtures cited, managers also will
have to create for themselves the appropriate mixture of D
and E. Before any learning or any movement toward the
proper balance can occur, the manager must agree to operate
within both frameworks, must agree that both modes are legitimate options. Creating this diversity mixture is an essential first step. For this, you will find the action choices of the
Diversity Paradigm a valuable approach.

Exclude (avoid):   This manager refuses to create the
                                      empowerment/doer mixture, per-
                                      haps because of philosophical pref-
                                      erences, a failure to perceive the

need for change, or an inability to commit to two approaches simultaneously.

Include: Accepts both frameworks as legitimate and commits to determine how to best use them.

Deny: Includes empowerment but disallows existence of significant differences between the two frameworks. "Both empowerment and doer management require respecting the individual and treating people fairly. We're doing this already." This perspective makes it unnecessary to talk about changing doer practices.

Isolate: Includes empowerment and sets it aside for special use, perhaps with the cream of the crop, minorities, women, or other specific groups. "I am using empowerment without changing mainstream 'doer' practices."

Suppress: Includes the empowerment framework and then allows it to slip from her day-to-day consciousness, perhaps because of philosophical incongruence or a sense that the corporation is not ready for this approach. This is the manager who undergoes empowerment training and does absolutely nothing with it.

Assimilate: Includes empowerment and implements those aspects that can be adapted to the doer approach. A good example is management by objectives (MBO). As defined by some theorists, MBO can be used as an empowerment tool where the individual identifies and negotiates his objectives. However, it is not uncommon to find doer managers who have assimilated this tool into their framework, dictating objectives to employees. This manager takes credit for empowering, even though he has compromised the tool through assimilation.

Tolerate: In this instance, does just enough through training and symbolic action to be perceived as having gotten on board the empowerment train. In reality, this manager never truly commits but simply tolerates empowerment. Minimum compliance, not commitment, is the order of the day.

Build relationships: Here, minimum compliance is combined with a lot of analysis and discussion that may or may not lead to committed action toward achieving a mixture of the two frameworks. At a minimum, managers are fluent in their understanding of both approaches.

Foster mutual adaptation: Commits to developing a framework with appropriate inclusions of the empowerment and doer approaches, with the relative proportions being a function of the manager's location in the hierarchy. In addition to having to address the diversity mixture of doer and empowerment frameworks, this individual must also relate to diversity mixtures concerned with learning and change. This is implicit in the notion of "mutual adaptation."

The Leadership Component

The second aspect of the managerial role is leadership—the process of ensuring that a corporation is positioned appropriately with respect to its external environment, so that long-term viability will be fostered. One quick way to appreciate the distinction between managing and leading is the time element: Managing is concerned with the short term; leading with issues requiring resolution over the long term.

Although the concept of leadership has been around for some time, only recently have corporations paid much attention to it in the true sense. Managers used to interchange leading and managing as if they were the same. Only after environmental shifts became sufficiently visible to suggest that at least some attention had to be given to the repositioning of corporations, did managers begin to differentiate between leading and managing. Another force driving the new focus on leadership is the decline in employees' passion and commitment. Leadership has become seen as a way of rekindling the passion of the workforce.

The Leadership Questions

Managers as leaders seek to understand the external environment, and then take steps to ensure that their organizations are positioned appropriately. Their activities focus on several questions:

 • *Do we have an appropriate mission?* In other words, does our purpose for existing fit environmental realities? If so, are the mission and its relationship to the external environment sufficiently understood by organizational participants? If not, what do I need to do to communicate the mission and its rationale effectively?

▪ *Do we have a vision?* Do we have an understanding and a picture of what would constitute successful achievement of our mission? If so, has the vision been sufficiently shared with organizational participants?

▪ *Do we have sufficient strategic-thinking and -planning capabilities?* Do we have the capability to devise an approach for securing and maintaining competitive advantage? If so, has that approach been imbued throughout the organization?

To understand this and the next question properly, please keep in mind that I am using the words *strategic* and *strategy* to describe those decisions made for the *express* purpose of gaining sustainable competitive advantage.[4]

▪ *Do we have a culture that is congruent with our external environment, mission, vision, and strategy?* By *culture*, I mean the basic assumptions that give rise to everything (cultural manifestations) that occurs in a corporation.[5] They were placed in existence by the founders and have been tested and refined repeatedly, so much so that they are taken for granted and become like the roots of a tree—out of sight but responsible for controlling everything in sight.[6]

The leadership task is to ensure that cultural modifications are made as needed to maintain congruence with the environment and with changes in mission, vision, and strategy.

Schematically, the relationships among the leadership variables and also between managing and leading are represented in Exhibit 4-2. For all these variables, the driving force is the environment.

This is why being able to accurately scan and understand environmental shifts is so critical. The leadership objective is to have a mission, vision, strategy, and culture that are indi-

Exhibit 4-2. Leadership/management framework.

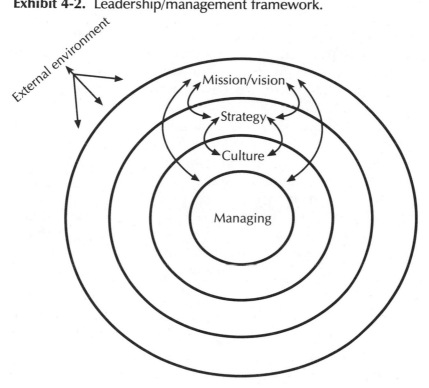

vidually congruent with each other, and collectively congruent with the external environment. Once this congruence is achieved, and *if* the environment remains stable, leadership relative to managing becomes unimportant. Because this was the case in the late 1960s, the 1970s, and perhaps the early 1980s in the United States, corporate leadership skills became rusty. Further, since most corporations have cultural roots that were put in place by their founders, few senior-level managers now have experience with culture change.

Now that corporate environments are viewed as dynamic, uncertain, and indeed destabilized, many corporations are searching for individuals who can lead (develop and communicate visions, think strategically, and modify cultures). To be viable in this setting, a corporation must have leadership *and* managerial capability.

Why Leadership Now?

In sum, leadership serves at least two critical purposes. First, it ensures that the fit between an enterprise and its external environment is viable. This is done by ensuring congruence between the external environment and an enterprise's mission, vision, strategy, and culture.

Second, leadership through mission, vision, strategy, and culture provides the vehicles through which employee commitment can evolve. Commitment is a condition where the individual is willing to go the extra mile—willing to give 200 percent to ensure achievement of the corporation's objectives. Commitment comes about when the individual's sources of meaning are compatible with the organization's. Both the individual and organization have a sense of what is important, of what gives meaning to life. The individual's sources of meaning derive from his basic assumptions about life, his values, predispositions, and attitudes; the organization's, from its culture, mission, vision, and strategy.[7]

A key task of the leadership portion of the managerial role is to raise the visibility of the organization's sources of meaning so that employees can compare their sources with those of the organization. The higher the congruence, the greater the individual's commitment will be. Ideally, where there is a lack of congruence, people will leave and seek compatibility in other organizations. As they go about their work of facilitating, coordinating, and problem solving, leaders are embedding the sources of meaning into the fabric of the organization. So leading is not an aloof, distant activity, but rather one that colors day-to-day issues.

Appropriate Balance of Leading and Managing

Just as the exercise of management involves finding a balance between doing and empowering, so doing the work of leading involves finding a balance between managing and leading. That balance task exists for the corporation as a whole, as well for the individual managers within it.

How large should a corporation's leadership capacity be relative to its managing capacity? For most corporations, the answer depends on the stability of their environment and the extent to which their managers subscribe to the inverse-pyramid assumption. The more dynamic and the more uncertain a corporation's environment, the greater will be the need for leadership capacity. Without a doubt, a corporation will always need strong management, but in white-water environments the need to tap the talent of 100 percent of your workforce is intensified. In dynamic environments, a corporation will need both capacities in substantial measure.

Each individual manager's role also has both components. In an environment characterized by uncertainty, the higher your position in the hierarchy, the larger your leadership component; conversely, the lower your standing in the hierarchy, the larger your management component (see Exhibit 4-3).

Coping With Change

Many corporate executives are just now becoming aware that leading and managing are not the same. Those making progress with "leadership" often encounter significant challenges.

Exhibit 4-3. The relative importance of leading and managing at various levels of the corporate pyramid.

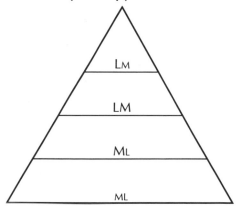

Some managers can generate visions without understanding how to imbue or embed them throughout their corporation. Others experience hang-ups on the "competitive advantage" aspect of strategic thinking. Finally, for most managers, the tasks of modifying and sustaining culture are especially challenging.

Applying the Diversity Paradigm

The challenges of securing appropriate leadership capability can be understood in the context of diversity mixtures. Managers face much the same complex situation as was described earlier in this chapter regarding the embracing of empowerment. In addition, they face the task of creating the appropriate mixture of leading and managing in themselves and in the overall organization. Once again, the Diversity Management precepts hold the answer.

Include/exclude:	Logic would suggest that leadership should be included, but nevertheless some managers exclude leadership because it is so different from management, in that it deals with issues related to the external environment and requires a relatively long-term perspective.
Deny:	This manager includes leadership, but then disallows the relevancy of vision, mission, strategy, and culture—the elements that differentiate leadership from management. This is the manager who hates the word *vision* or believes that its importance has been overstated, or who downplays the critical nature of anything that is "soft." A critical difference between the denying

manager and the one who excludes is that the excluding manager understands leadership and consciously decides to exclude, while the denying manager includes leadership but never really gets in touch with what it means.

Isolate: Includes leadership and sets it apart as something special and almost mystical. This manager talks about the "art" of leading, visioning, strategic thinking, and changing culture. He is saying that this should be part of his diversity mixture, but because of the "artsy" nature should be left primarily to those with the unique talent. In some situations, the setting-aside is based on the assumption that leadership is reserved as a function of the most senior executives. The thinking here is that the manager will establish the diversity mixture of leadership and management but not deal with leadership until he acquires the "art" or assumes a senior managerial position. Obviously, this posture excuses him from having to deal seriously with leadership. This individual is prepared to play only a minor support role with respect to the leadership function.

Suppress: Includes leadership but removes whatever she learns about it from her consciousness. The causal factor for this manager may be the

	pressures of the moment, perceived lack of readiness on the part of the manager or corporation, or simply a lack of conceptual clarity. In any event, the leadership component is inactive and not in the manager's day-to-day thinking.
Assimilate:	Includes leadership and then assimilates it into management. This manager relates only to those aspects of leadership that can be described, correctly or incorrectly, as "management." Because this individual has a high level of "management," a very low level of "leadership," and a short-term orientation, he will see culture as something that can be changed overnight and strategy as a short-term issue.
Tolerate:	Includes but does not embrace leadership and consciously downplays it. This manager is aware of the leadership concept, but consciously decides to do little with it. If necessary, he can converse skillfully and thoughtfully about the topic, but will fail to take any significant action.
Build relationships:	Actively and vigorously seeks to understand leadership and management as they relate to each other and the organization. This intense exploration can be a prelude to significant mutual adaptation, or it can become a substitute for change.
Foster mutual adaptation:	Understands the complexity of

leadership and management individually and moves to adopt a more complex model that allows him to engage in both. He develops a complex framework for action that encompasses both leadership and management and also both the doer and empowerment modes of management.

Finding the Path

In this chapter we are talking about nothing less than the essence of management and of leadership. Several conclusions present themselves:

1. *The prescriptions described in this chapter are demanding:* Achieve conceptual understanding of leadership and management, strike appropriate balances between doing and empowering and between managing and leading, develop the skill to adjust balances on a contingency basis, and practice facilitating empowerment and leadership. This is a lot to ask of one person and probably contributes to the reality of limited sustainable progress.

2. *The concepts are complex.* Even for one experienced with the writing of business thinkers, ferreting out and integrating meanings and nuances can be a challenge. For a doer manager not oriented toward reflection and the long term, this could be a challenge that further compromises progress.

3. *Implementation is complex.* For many managers it will require massive shifts involving several diversity mixtures for individuals and organizations. This is exactly the kind of complicated, long-term change that is most difficult for doer managers.

4. *Given those realities, it is not practical to expect one person to carry the principal responsibility for both managing and leading.*

Instead, it is more practical and accurate to talk of the "management function" and the "leadership function," where managers at all levels contribute to both in differing proportions.

I am reminded here of a minister friend of mine who was visiting in a city where he was scheduled to be a guest preacher a few weeks later. On this early visit, he decided to drive to the church so he could learn the route. He found the church with no problem and went inside. It was midafternoon on a weekday, and no one was in sight but the custodian. My friend introduced himself, and they began to chat. With little or no prompting, the custodian delivered a one-hour monologue on the church's mission and vision. It was clear he wanted to be sure the soon-to-be guest minister would have the appropriate context for preparing his sermon. In this organization, the mission and vision had been imbued throughout the congregation, and that custodian, by addressing himself to mission and vision, was as much a leader as anyone in the hierarchy.

5. *Without a doubt, facility with the Diversity Management process would make it easier to deal with the diversity and complexity reflected in conclusions 1 through 4.* It would enhance the individual's capacity to understand the multiple dimensions of management and leadership and to act appropriately even when those dimensions contradict each other. Without this capability, progress will be limited.

6. *Conversely, substantial management and leadership capabilities are major prerequisites for utilizing the Diversity Management process.* If progress cannot be made and sustained with respect to both aspects of the managerial role, progress with the Diversity Management process will be even more difficult.

5

Black, White, and Shades of Gray: "People" Diversity

While this book focuses on diversity mixtures other than the workforce, this does not mean we cannot learn by applying the process to the setting we traditionally have targeted. Indeed, examining the familiar through a different lens—the Diversity Management process—can be illuminating, so let's turn our attention to the workforce.

In 1984, when I founded the American Institute for Managing Diversity (AIMD), I was motivated by several observations.

The first was that managers and organizations were experiencing limited success in retaining and promoting minorities and women. They were clustered disproportionately at the bottom of corporate pyramids, and often were leaving corporations after encountering career stagnation.[1] Those who stayed worked in a climate of unhappiness, either resigned to or disappointed about their status.

My second observation was that the traditional explanation of white male bias did not always apply. Even managers with good intentions and minimal bias were having difficulty retaining and promoting minorities and women. They were frustrated not only with their lack of success but with the lack of credit they were given for their good-faith efforts.

I also noted that managers were increasingly disillusioned with affirmative action as a remedy. Many had experienced several episodes of the same frustrating cycle: intense

efforts to recruit minorities and women, disappointing reten-
tion and mobility rates for members of these groups, renewed
recruitment efforts, and continued inability to retain members of the targeted groups or to facilitate their upper mobility.[2]

As I talked to managers, I found that most of them had
a pet theory on what was needed. Typically, these theories,
based on anecdotal evidence rather than systematic thinking
or diagnosis, called for efforts to "fix" minorities and women,
relieve white males of bias, and improve communications
and interpersonal relationships. But even managers with
these theories were not optimistic.

One observation struck me as most significant: Few managers were exploring the possibility of changing their organizations to meet these challenges. The emphasis was on fixing
individuals or groups. This realization led me to begin evolving AIMD's version of Managing Diversity.

Essentially, in 1984, two approaches existed for addressing workforce diversity, affirmative action and understanding differences. I proposed a third, Managing Diversity,
which I defined as "a comprehensive managerial process for
developing an environment that works for all employees."[3]

By articulating the ideas of Managing Diversity more
than a decade ago, I was calling for enhanced *organizational
capability* with respect to minorities and women. I was saying
that we needed to adjust corporate cultures, values, systems,
processes, and climates to ensure that they enabled *all* employees to reach their potential in pursuit of company objectives. This was especially important because minorities and
women had not been factored into the development of these
organizational parameters.

Sadly, in the ten years since, I have seen little change.
Organizations still do not work well for nontraditional workers. Recruitment and utilization of minorities and women remain problematic for most enterprises. The progress that has
been made with upper mobility for minorities and women
has come about through deliberate and concentrated efforts,

rather than through the "natural" operations of corporations. Popular corporate wisdom, for example, contends that much progress has been made with respect to retaining and promoting white women. Yet conversations with white women reveal that the processes that have allowed this to happen have often gone against the organizational grain.

Blaming lack of progress on white-male bias still, in my mind, does not capture the totality of the problem. Over the ten years of my work with AIMD, I have seen many well-intentioned, relatively bias-free white males fail in the diversity arena. One white-male manager, attending a seminar with a diverse group of participants, wailed in frustration, "Tell me what to do. I don't deny the issues you raise, but I don't know what to do." The others shouted back angrily, "You don't ask us how to fix other challenges. Why are you all of a sudden at a loss for action?" Both sides left the session angry and disappointed.

Dissatisfaction with affirmative action has increased. Calls for significant changes abound, as do arguments that affirmative action be abolished. White males perceive it as reverse discrimination against them, often on behalf of "unqualified minorities and women."[4] For their part, minorities and women complain loudly too. They say that affirmative action stigmatizes "qualified" minorities and women who would have been hired on their own merits, and compromises their credibility and ability to move up the organizational ladder.[5]

Finally, managers persist in pursuing their pet theories—striving to fix minorities and women, relieve white males of their biases, and facilitate harmonious communications and understanding. They are still focused at the individual or group level and continue to neglect serious consideration of *organizational modifications* to reflect diversity realities.

Managers, in general, are not using comprehensive solution processes in the diversity arena. Evidence that this is true can be seen in the similarity between much of what is being said about diversity in the 1990s and what was said in the 1960s and 1970s.

I still hear, for example, "We need to do a better job attracting and recruiting minorities and women." This reference to *targeted recruitment efforts* aimed at minorities and women dates back to the 1960s. I also hear of seminars designed to "help white men get in touch with their biases, so they will be comfortable with other people." *Efforts to minimize white male bias* can be traced back at least to the early 1970s.

Managers continue to talk about *facilitating the assimilation of minorities and women.* Typically, such conversations focus on the need to "do a better job of helping minorities and women understand the requirements for success—to help them understand how corporations work and what adjustments they will have to make to fit in." Again, these concerns date back to the 1970s.

Managers also talk of *developing role models* by recruiting minorities and women for high-level positions. This recruitment is based on the belief that "minorities and women need role models showing that they too can be successful" and on the attendant hope that these imported "role models" will facilitate the companies' efforts to grow their own. This school of thought, like the others, can be traced back to at least the seventies. Finally, managers continue to report on *fostering mentoring relationships* where white males mentor minorities. This, too, is a seventies solution.

What's new is that these approaches, which originated in the sixties and seventies, are now used under the label of "diversity." The pros and cons of each can be debated. The question is not whether they can produce progress under certain circumstances but why the progress they produce is not sustainable. Yet, few managers raise—let alone address—this question. Further, labeling these efforts as diversity creates conceptual confusion as to what diversity and Managing Diversity are about.

What's also new is the continuing reality of downsizing

and the uncertainty it creates. This reality has not only exacerbated the frustrations and disappointment of many minorities and women; it has created doubts about the possibility of future progress as well.

It's reasonable to ask why, given all the talk about diversity over the past ten years, we have not seen greater progress. One reason may be that managers really have not addressed diversity, Managing Diversity, or Diversity Management as we have defined these concepts in this book. Instead, they have allowed their traditional understanding and experiences with race and gender to define their perceptions of diversity. That is, they have interpreted workforce diversity to mean race and gender diversity only. This has led them to conclude that diversity, Managing Diversity, and Diversity Management all equate to affirmative action, which puts the onus of change on individuals or groups.

Another reason for the lack of progress is that even when managers understand and attempt to move forward with Managing Diversity, the process is long-term. Those few managers who are adopting this approach are in the early stages of education and diagnosis, where limited progress would be expected.

A third reason for the lack of progress, and perhaps the most significant, is an inadequate understanding of complexity—diversity's sidekick. This limited understanding can lead to misunderstandings about what is going on, and that in turn can lead to managers' offering "solutions" to the wrong problem.

What is essential is for managers to understand the scope and impact of diversity and its inevitable consequence, complexity.

The Complexity Factor

Diversity and Complexity

Diversity generates complexity in terms of multiplicity and variations.[6] One way to think about this is to imagine that you are juggling three balls and you are quite good at it. Your boss comes along and says that you are now required to juggle five. Clearly, this makes your task more complex. At a minimum, you will need greater hand speed.

While you are learning to increase hand speed, your boss informs you that you will be juggling five *objects*, not five balls, and that these objects will differ in size, shape, and weight. This further complicates your juggling life. Not only will you need greater hand speed; you will also need to vary your grip for the different objects, and to take into account the varying weights to anticipate the speeds with which the objects will move through the air. You must make several calculations and adjustments simultaneously.

How well you can do this depends on how well you can handle complexity. If these simultaneous adjustments are beyond your complexity capability, you will experience frustration and failure. If these circumstances persist, you may learn to dislike those objects that are so different from the balls you were once comfortable with and are contributing to your current difficulty.

Diversity creates complexity, which, in turn, presents challenges for all individuals and creates resentments within those with limited capacity for complexity. In truth, most of us prefer to avoid complexity, which means avoiding diversity.

In work with corporations of all types, I have witnessed this preference many times. It was evident in the manager who admonished me to introduce diversity concepts to his organization through the KISS (Keep It Simple, Stupid) formula. It was also evident in the manager who reacted to a discussion on permanent white water by saying, "We must remember that the rank and file prefer the known to the unknown, the certain to the uncertain, and the predictable to the unpredictable. We must always give them assurances." I responded by asking, "What if you cannot give assurances? Suppose you are not in control of the permanent white water?" The manager replied, "You still have to give assurances."

This preference for simplicity is evident in managers who depend on quantitative data and refuse to consider nonquantitative information. It is further evident in organizations that categorize their managers as "task-oriented" or "people-oriented"—implying that no manager can do both. These managers don't deny the benefits of addressing the dimension they are ignoring; they just don't see any reason to complicate their lives by dealing with tasks *and* people. Theirs is a pragmatic decision to minimize complexity as much as possible.

This may seem reasonable, but it has a very dangerous outcome: When people succeed in minimizing complexity, they hinder the development of a capability to manage it. Since diversity is part and parcel of complexity, they limit their ability to manage diversity as well. That has profound implications for anyone concerned with employee performance.

Complexity and Workforce Bias

Without a doubt, we can look at Organization America and see that a significant amount of workforce behavior has an impact that is discriminatory on the basis of something other than merit. Also without a doubt, bias of any kind is counterproductive in a business setting. Bias is usually deeply rooted, even unconscious; it is not always easy to understand, harder still to eliminate. I believe that the concept of complexity can be of great value here:

1. *A limited ability to deal with complexity can lead to bias.* I have a great comfort level with people of my race. Placing me in an environment where there are multiple races complicates my life. If I am unable to modify my "juggling process" to address this complexity, I will experience frustration. It's possible that I will develop an "attitude" toward people whose

behaviors are beyond my complexity capability. This attitude may lead me to exclude, attack, or stereotype these individuals. The driver of my bias is my limited ability to deal with complexity.

2. *Behavior that appears to be driven by bias may instead be driven by a limited ability to deal with complexity, or by a combination of the two.* Even if an organization could somehow achieve a bias-free state, we would probably still see biaslike behavior among its members if the managers of that organization remained limited in their ability to address complexity. The managers' inability to design an organization with sufficient complexity capability to match the complexity of the workforce would result in biaslike behavior. This proposition has serious implications. It suggests that success in eliminating bias may not, in itself, lead to organization environments that can empower a diverse workforce.

3. *The drive to eliminate biaslike behavior and to empower the total workforce must be expanded to include efforts to enhance capability to deal with complexity.* This proposition neither denies nor minimizes the importance of fighting racism, sexism, and other "isms." Efforts against the "isms" should be continued and indeed intensified. However, we should complement these endeavors with strategies for enhancing complexity capability on the part of employees, managers, and organizations. The explicit purpose of Diversity Management is not to reduce bias but rather to foster utilization of employee potential. Yet the process can lead to enhanced capability to deal with complexity, which, in addition to producing movement toward full utilization of a diverse workforce, can bring about minimization of bias and the reduction of biaslike behavior. This is particularly important in light of some major changes in the traditional individual-organizational relationship, examined later in this chapter.

The Diversity Management process can provide a context for addressing the complexity associated with any diverse mixture. What follows is a demonstration of how the Diversity Paradigm, a component of Diversity Management, can be used with mixtures relating to workforce diversity.

Influenced again by the notion that looking at the familiar through different lenses can be illuminating, I selected race as our focus of analysis. It is one, if not *the* one, of the workforce diversity dimensions with which we frequently have been most interested.

Race and the Diversity Action Options

Before people can use Diversity Management process with respect to race, they must acknowledge that racial differences exist. For some, this recognition presents substantial challenges.

Some find the notion of racial differences difficult because their experiences across races suggest that "people are people" regardless of race. Therefore, they believe that the best guideline for interracial interactions is to follow the Golden Rule: Treat others as you would have them treat you.

People who embrace humanitarianism may also resist recognizing differences. This philosophy emphasizes the developmental potential of all people and affirms each individual's dignity, worth, and capacity for self-realization. It downplays differences among people. A manager who subscribes to this philosophy, for example, holds that all employees have self-actualization potential.[7]

Those who believe strongly that all people are creatures of a Supreme Creator also tend to minimize differences. Their belief that all "children of the Creator" are equal leads them to assert that all races are the same.

Others stifle their ability to see racial differences in their desire to be race- or color-blind. This race-blindness may spring from societal preference or from personal necessity. Some people say, in effect, "If I allow myself to acknowledge that you are from a different race or culture, I may punish you for not being like me. By being race-blind, I'm doing you a favor and protecting you from an attack by me."

A few years ago, I had a personal encounter with race-blindness. During a discussion period following my presentation on diversity, a high-ranking white executive noted how difficult it is to work with black males, given that all the black males he sees are on the evening news on their way to jail. He made this statement looking directly at me, a black male. "Hell," I responded, "you haven't seen *me* on the evening news." I was admonishing him not to stereotype me. The manager looked at me and smiled, as if getting in touch with an insight.

I now realize that I misread the situation. The executive was not stereotyping me; he simply refused to see me as a black male. He clearly knew I was not a white male, but he categorized me as something other than black. And it was to my advantage that he did so. Had he not been race-blind with respect to me, he would have treated me in keeping with his attitude toward the black men he had seen on television. His race-blind stance protected both me and him from his stereotyping thinking and behavior.

Finally, there are some individuals who do deny racial differences because they do not find the construct of race to be socially useful or scientifically valid. They note that racial diversity includes multiple races, not just black and white. They also note that certain ethnic groups do not fall neatly into the usual categories of white, black, Asian, American, Hispanic, and Native Americans. For example, Latinos—often referred to as Hispanics—are neither a race nor an ethnic group, but a disparate collection of nationalities variously descended from Europeans, African slaves, and American Indians. The complexity of the racial diversity mixture has convinced these individuals that it is foolish to use race as a way to categorize.

Yet to refuse to accept racial differences as a reality is to be out of step with the rest of the world. Most Americans act as if racial differences are real and significant. My observations of corporate America have convinced me that race—or more specifically, one's belief about race—does matter. The collective beliefs about race get played out within organizations each day.

The blunt question we must all face is, what can we do about it? In this most delicate of issues, where people of goodwill are often baffled, I believe the Diversity Management process, specifically the Diversity Paradigm, offers a way of objective analysis.

Let us see how this might work. In the sections that follow, the Diversity Paradigm is applied to racial diversity from three perspectives: managers, employees who are members of racial minorities, and white males. The discussion assumes a recognition and acceptance of racial differences, or at least a desire to explore the complexities associated with race. It also assumes that even those individuals who don't acknowledge racial differences need a way of thinking about and behaving within settings where people act as if they are real.

The Managerial Perspective

In all likelihood, today's managers will find themselves responsible for facilitating the performance of a racially diverse group, many, if not most, of them racially different from themselves. Managers with limited interracial experience can find this mixture intimidating: What can I expect from members of this race? How do I facilitate their efforts? How different are members of the various races? How do I make sure we all get along? Is it really true what I've heard about members of this race? How will they relate to me? All these questions and others must be addressed in the midst of other work-related complexities.

Managerial options for addressing racial diversity and coping with complexity in pursuit of organizational objectives can be framed by the Diversity Paradigm:

Include/exclude

Since it is legally and politically unacceptable to exclude individuals solely because of their race, or conversely to hire people because of race, managers generally do not have these options.

Deny:

Race-blindness is the principal vehicle here. Hoping to minimize complexity and divisiveness, this manager neither recognizes racial groupings nor encourages racial references. He will be likely to discourage such innovations as racial support groups and special days celebrating the experiences of a particular race.

The denial option has been popular until relatively recently, but changing attitudes are making denial increasingly difficult. Employees more and more are willing to be categorized by race when they deem it appropriate, even if it means they will be viewed as different. They are also increasingly comfortable with indicating when traditional racial designations do not apply. The enhanced comfort level with racial complexity makes managerial denial less possible.

Isolate:

Opts to isolate the different groupings in an attempt to sort through the racial complexity. This reduces complexity and allows this manager to deal with workers of different races separately without disrupting the order of the dominant racial group—typically white males.

A key vehicle for achieving this isolation has been stereotyping. It allows the manager to assign each racial group a niche in which behavior is predictable. Once the manager labels someone as a member of a given racial group, his stereotypes offer a basis for predicting that person's behavior. This reduces the complexity that the manager must address.

The problem with this is that as people become comfortable in being different, managers are not managing groups but individuals. Increasing variations within racial groupings make racial designations less valid and indeed less useful as predictors of behavior. Stereotypes are exposed for what they are: assumptions about groups that may not apply to individuals.

Suppress: Seeks to minimize diversity and complexity by requiring individuals to suppress "racial manifestations" while at work. This manager recognizes race and may even overtly condone racial pride—but not at work. Away from work, he may attend festivals, dinners, and dances where racial attributes are celebrated, but he asks employees to suppress their ethnic dress, language, music, or food preferences while they are at work. This man-

Assimilate:

ager often earns a reputation as culturally sensitive while minimizing complexity and preserving the integrity of the traditional workforce. Minimizes or eliminates complexity by requiring assimilation. This manager articulates the prevailing way of doing business, and works to fit everyone to this ideal. Historically, assimilation has been a preferred action option for minimizing complexity. But assimilation has its limits. This is where the notion of "true requirements" comes into play.

Typically, managers who push for assimilation speak of the organizations's "requirements" as if they were absolutes, when in fact most "requirements" also include preferences, conveniences, and traditions. The corporate mold, comprising true requirements and also these preferences, traditions, and conveniences, was developed sometime in the past, by whatever race was dominant then. People who are racially different from that dominant race may find it difficult to assimilate, especially in relation to traditions and preferences. In some instances, assimilation is impossible as, for example, when there is a "preference requirement" that employees be white.

Changing attitudes show up here too; the more people become com-

Tolerate:

fortable with being different, the less likely they are to accept unnecessary assimilation.

Endorses pluralism and declares that room exists in the workplace for all races. Sometimes this manager's tolerance is a reluctant response to equal opportunity and affirmative action efforts.

With the toleration option, references to race and racial differences are commonplace and the comfort level with racial issues is relatively high. Yet while there is room for all races, all are not equal. The dominant racial grouping remains in place and remains dominant; the status quo is preserved. Minorities feel welcome but not fully accepted as participants. They are painfully aware of their "tolerated" status and talk frequently about the need to "value diversity." Valuing diversity here means "accept all of us fully," or "do not treat me as an affirmative action hire who is not qualified." To be tolerated is to be kept in limbo between full participation and exclusion.

Build relationships:

With this option, management fosters acceptance and understanding across races. Priority is placed on establishing quality relationships, with the assumption that good relations will lead to a harmonious climate that can provide a context for enhanced productivity. Activities celebrating the culture of the various races are the norm.

A consequence of these efforts can be that relationships are genuinely harmonious, but minorities continue to feel they do not truly belong because organizational parameters remain unchanged. The result is a racially diverse population with good relationships within an organization whose parameters are not designed with diversity in mind. Complexity is minimized by harmonious relationships—but only up to a point. The organization level remains incongruous with the realities of diversity and complexity. This phase can set the stage for mutual adaptation.

Foster mutual adaptation: Here complexity is addressed through adaptation by both parties. The governing criterion is true requirements. The key questions are, what does the organization require from the individual, and what does the individual require from the organization?

By focusing only on true requirements and pushing individual and organizational preferences, conveniences, and traditions to the side, the parties identify the essentials for the relationship and free up room for negotiations around the nonrequirements. This movement by both parties allows assimilation where it is necessary for organizational requirements and also some flexibility in other areas where the individual is comfortable with being different. Mutual adaptation implicitly entails the possibility of changing organizational parameters.

The action options offer the manager alternatives for harnessing diversity and complexity in pursuit of corporate objectives. If managers cannot work with a mixture of multiple races with significant variations among and within themselves, the performance of their units will suffer.

The Minorities Perspective

Minorities have at least three sets of complexities to address. One is the racial diversity between the minority employee and her boss. "How does my boss feel toward people of my race? Is she prejudiced? What does she know about people like me? What have been her experiences with my race? Has she ever promoted anyone like me? How different are we from each other?"

Another is the racial diversity of peers. This can be a sea of faces reflecting enormous racial diversity. "Who are these people? What is the nature of their cultures? Are they racist? Can we work together? How did these 'different' people get here? What do they know about me?"

The third set of complexities involves intraracial issues. The minority person looks around for members of his race, but then discovers that all members of his race are not the same: "They look like me, but are they? What are their backgrounds? Do we have anything in common? Can I trust them to be supportive? Do the males and females within the race get along? Are they more 'white' than minority? How do the nonmanagerial minorities relate to minorities who are managers?"

The Diversity Paradigm offers minority employees a framework for sorting out these complexities.

Include/exclude (join/avoid):   There are few settings of signifi-
cant size where the individual can avoid racial diversity in the workforce. So the choice of join-ing or not joining such a mixture does not usually exist.

Deny: People who use denial refuse to see differences or to consider them important. They often make comments such as: "We're all humans. I don't see any real differences." "We're all God's children." "If you really get to know people, they're all the same. Race is irrelevant."

Denial minimizes complexity substantially by grouping all people together and reducing race to insignificance. This ap-proach can be used with all three sets of issues: boss-subordinate, peers, and intraracial.

Isolate: Here the minority employee may elect isolation with respect to his boss whenever possible because of insecurity about his standing with her. The employee mini-mizes the complexity of the rela-tionship by minimizing contact. He focuses on his responsibilities and, when possible, works inde-pendently of the boss. These iso-lation practices, adopted some-times as a way of demonstrating competency and independence, can lead to severance—the ultimate isolation.

With peers, the employee brings order to his complexity by isolating through stereotyping. This allows him to act as if group stereotypes will prejudice individual behavior, and thus to minimize discomfort and uncertainty.

Isolation through stereotyping can also be used to order intraracial relations. All kinds of labels can be used to group and stereotype within minority races: managerial minorities, nonmanagerial minorities, minorities who live in *the* section of the city, minorities who went to prestige schools, minorities who went to nonprestige schools, minorities who have been here since the company's birth, minorities who have just arrived. With each label goes a set of stereotypical assumptions that simplify the individual's complexity. The challenge with stereotyping, of course, is that it can lead to behavior that is incongruent with reality.

Suppress: Minorities can suppress racial manifestations that may not play well with their boss or peers. Some minorities who choose suppression lead two very different lives, going back and forth between them every day. Because different suppressions are needed for the different mixtures, these individuals risk considerable stress and even emotional problems. The reduction of complexity is achieved at a considerable price.

Assimilate: Here the individual seeks to minimize complexity by becoming like the dominant race in the organization. She adopts the dress, personality, mannerisms, work practices, residential location, and automobile type of these colleagues. If the boss is a member of the dominant racial group, the individual tries to become a clone of the manager. The hope is that assimilation will lead not only to a less complicated relationship but perhaps to a promotion as well.

Assimilation, like suppression, cannot be used simultaneously in all three settings. Unless minority peers are heavily into assimilation themselves, successful assimilation with the manager and toward the dominant racial ideal is likely to alienate the individual from a substantial number of those within her race.

Assimilation does, undoubtedly, reduce complexity. But it conflicts with the growing trend toward increased comfort in being different. Adopting this option requires the individual to come to grips with the implications for her sense of identity and self-worth.

Tolerate: "Live and let live" is the philosophy here. The individual agrees that all races have a legitimate right to participate in the workforce and is willing, in effect, to "go along to get along." But he connects only marginally with members of other races, and limits even this connection to the work setting. He complies with the need to work with everyone but has little commitment to or enthusiasm for the process. This lukewarm approach avoids the complexity that would be associated with intimate relationships.

Employees can choose to relate to their boss with the "tolerate" option; this involves complying with the boss's agenda so they can get along and receive a promotion. Under this option, the boss-subordinate relationship is one step more intense and intimate than with isolation, but still very loose; neither commitment nor intimacy is part of the picture.

With racial peers, "tolerate" results in a shallow relationship with minimum bonding or support. The relevant questions often remain unanswered because of the superficiality of the relationship. Yet there is little bickering within the race, in part because there is no serious discussion.

Build relationships:

The individual opts to establish relationships with her boss, peers, and minority peers, perhaps in the belief that relationships can facilitate accomplishments. This option does not require that any party change. It calls, instead, for relationships characterized by greater acceptance, understanding, bonding intensity, and intimacy. Celebrations of racial cultures and the appearance of support groups, for example, are likely.

The individual seeks to foster acceptance and understanding between her boss and herself, and between herself and peers of the same and different races. The result can be a harmonious relationship where all parties are comfortable in talking about the racial complexity and diversity they share.

Foster mutual adaptation:

The individual is willing to adapt, to make changes for the sake of creating effective relationships. His boss, peers, and racial peers are also prepared to change. Once again, the focus is on true requirements. With the organization as a whole, and with peers and racial peers, the emphasis is on developing the kind of relationships that will facilitate accomplishment of organizational objectives.

What becomes clear is that the more comfortable individuals become in being different, the more likely they are to choose toleration, building relationships, or mutual adaptation as their action options. The last two, in particular, encourage expectations based on requirements, not power differentials, traditions, preferences, or conveniences.

The White-Male Perspective

White males now find themselves sharing workplaces that historically they have dominated—a circumstance of significant complexity. Reactions to this racial diversity have ranged from warm welcomes and reluctant acceptance to condescension, fear, and outright backlash. Some of the negative reactions must be attributed to racism, but others can be traced to a limited ability to deal with complexity.

Here again, the Diversity Paradigm provides a framework for understanding the white-male response. Relevant questions include: How do these people from different races feel about white males? Will they try to do to me what they claim my predecessors did to their predecessors? Will they push for preferential treatment? Are they like the media portraits of their races? Where do they come from? Does this mean white males are no longer wanted or valued?

Join/avoid (include/exclude): The option of joining workforces not characterized by racial diversity is limited. Most white males and employees in general have

little choice but to find themselves in the midst of racial diversity.

Deny:
Here the white male refuses to
recognize racial differences, for a
variety of previously mentioned
reasons and also in an effort to
preserve the status quo. Where
denial prevails, it is unnecessary
to talk about the need for major
changes in interpersonal relationships and organizational parameters.

Isolate:
The white male uses isolation
through stereotyping as a way of
sorting through the complexity
created by racial diversity. This
does, in fact, simplify his life and
keep him from becoming overwhelmed. But it also can lead to
poor decisions if the group assumptions do not fit individual
realities.

Suppress:
While on the job, the white male
suppresses prejudicial beliefs or
behaviors that would offend his
managers or his racially diverse
peers. As a result, he, like the minority employee who uses suppression, lives in two worlds,
going back and forth between
them every day.

Suppression of "politically incorrect" behavior minimizes conflict and complexity at work, but
it complicates the white male's
life in general. Hiding the gap

Assimilate:

between how he must behave at work and who he really is creates great stress and resentment.

In organizations where Diversity Management is truly being practiced, assimilation becomes less attractive for the white male. An assimilation model based on true requirements often eliminates the traditions and preferences that white males are used to. A common result is backlash. These males suppress their discontent at work and surface it away from work, especially in political settings. Backlash may be, but is not necessarily, bias-driven. It can be caused by difficulty in adjusting to change and a limited ability to deal with complexity. Without a structured way to think about change and complexity with respect to race, white-male backlash may become more substantial.

Tolerate:

Here, the white male reluctantly accepts the reality that his work life will be complicated by racial diversity. He minimizes the complexity by opting for superficial, minimum relationships reflecting a "live and let live" attitude. He complies with expectations, suppresses inappropriate thoughts and behaviors, and does what is needed to ensure viable relationships with racially

	diverse peers. He looks good on the outside, but his heart is not in it. This explains why, despite the obvious increase in workforce diversity and the relative absence of racial conflict in the workplace, minorities still plead for diversity to be valued and white males still complain about political correctness.
Build relationships:	The white male buys into the importance of relationships and moves to foster increased acceptance and understanding across races. He wants to know and be known better by a variety of "others." The result can be harmonious relationships that minimize the possibility of racial slurs or conflict. His relationships with members of his own and other racial groups reflect a level of intimacy and cooperation that can spill over beyond work.
Foster mutual adaptation:	Responding to the business requirements for success and the reality of racial diversity, the white male accepts the need for change and participates in designing and implementing change at several levels: individual, interpersonal, group, and organization. This mutual adaptation is absolutely necessary if we are to create an environment and organization that empower *all* employees regardless of race.

One consistent thread connecting all the perspectives presented is an inability to talk about complexity and racial issues. In fact, our interactions with corporations suggest indeed that both white males and minorities are opting for suppression; white males suppress their frustration and channel it into their nonwork environment, while minorities suppress their concerns and code them in pleas for "valuing diversity." The net consequence is that critical issues simply are not on the table.

This failure to communicate feeds on itself. White males do not want to be viewed as politically incorrect, and minorities hesitate to be seen as complainers. So both look for safe avenues of expressions, while unexpressed tension builds at the work site. Part of the problem is that up to now, we have not had a systematic process for discussing racial diversity. Diversity Management offers a potential remedy, in that it provides a framework for diversity to define race, rather than the other way around.

Improving Communications Around Race

How can communications around racial issues be enhanced? Given our analyses from the perspective of managers, minorities, and white males, this question becomes key. Progress in this brings productivity gains. In this section we explore how the Diversity Management process can be used to improve one critical relationship, that between the manager (representing the organization) and individual members of a diverse workforce. This individual-organization relationship has been called a "psychological contract." I will draw upon insights from this concept to facilitate application of the Diversity Management process.

Nature of the Psychological Contract

The relationship between the individual employee and the organization, embodied in that employee's manager, is built on a set of reciprocal expectations. Each party seeks to establish a relationship because of what it expects to gain in exchange for what it gives to the other party. Those mutual expectations make up a contract of sorts between employee and organization, a psychological contract.[8]

For example, the individual may expect to receive and the organization may expect to give:

1. Salary
2. Personal development opportunities
3. Recognition and approval for good work
4. Security through fringe benefits
5. Friendly, supportive environment
6. Fair treatment
7. Meaningful or purposeful job

In turn, the individual may expect to give and the organization may expect to receive:

1. An honest day's work
2. Loyalty to organization
3. Initiative
4. Conformity to organizational norms
5. Job effectiveness
6. Flexibility and a willingness to learn and to develop

The manager's objective is to develop a contract that has a "fit" between what the manager expects to give and receive and what the individual expects to give and receive. When this is achieved, commitment is maximized because individuals can simultaneously fulfill organizational expectations while satisfying their own.

It is no easy task. The contract is, for several reasons, a fragile one. For one thing, some of the expectations are clearly articulated, while some are unstated. Both parties are bound by the verbalized and nonverbalized aspects of the contract. Matters are complicated by the fact that the contract is not between two individuals, but between an individual and an organization.

More difficult still is the fact that the needs and expectations of the individual and the organization are dynamic. They change over time and as circumstances and priorities vary. When the employee's needs change, the usual solution is for that person to leave and search for a better fit elsewhere. When the organization's needs change, the usual solution is some measure of layoffs. In these days of downsizing—or rightsizing, as some call the process—the broken contract is common.

It is to everyone's advantage to explicitly renegotiate the contract periodically. In white-water environments, it is critical.

Renegotiating the Contract

If managers are to engage today's diverse workforce and secure their commitment, they will have to establish viable contracts that reflect complexity and diversity. Diversity Management can serve both sides as a jointly shared framework for negotiating psychological contracts congruent with white-water realities.

In this section are guidelines for establishing such contracts. Recommendations are presented from the manager's perspective.

Preparation for Negotiation

1. Foster an understanding of environmental realities by both parties and help them to understand that any contract must be congruent with these realities.

2. Foster adoption of a mutually endorsed and shared process, such as the Diversity Management process, for discussing and thinking about diversity and complexity. This would make it possible to consider issues related to various diversity mixtures, including racial diversity.

3. Have both the manager and the employee practice using the Diversity Management process with nonsensitive topics before progressing to more sensitive ones. This will foster trust between the parties and in the process itself.

4. Foster understanding of and commitment to the organization's mission, vision, strategy, and culture in the context of environmental realities.

5. Encourage the differentiation of requirements from preferences, traditions, and conveniences. This, too, should be done before the negotiation session as it relates directly to understanding environmental realities, as well as to the organization's mission, vision, strategy, and culture. Clearly, the Diversity Management process will be helpful here.

6. Signal the desired action options on critical issues. For example, with respect to racial diversity, the manager should indicate where he would like the employee to focus; if he wants the department to move beyond suppression, he should indicate this before negotiations start.

7. Foster reflection. Individuals who wish to participate meaningfully in contract negotiation must first be in tune with who they are, whom they wish to become, and how they will get there. Without this self-reflection, commitment to viable psychological contracts will be limited.

Similarly, managers must reflect on the nature of the organization, its aspirations, and its plans for realizing its goals. This reflection is a critical part of the preparation process.

Negotiation

8. Avoid confusing contract negotiations with setting performance goals or giving performance feedback. Contract negotiations establish the broad parameters of the relationship, which in turn provide the context for setting specific performance objectives. Contract and performance-oriented sessions should be kept separate.

9. Expect the employee's buy-in on the organization's mission, vision, strategy, and culture; it is the foundation of

individual commitment. Securing true buy-in is part of the manager's leadership function and takes place over a period of time.

10. Incorporate the core requirements in the contract. These requirements should be specified in detail and should affirm the unit's mission, vision, strategy, and culture.

11. Take care to encourage expression of individual expectations and to incorporate them explicitly in the contract. The relationship is two-way. The manager who is unclear about the individual's expectations cannot be clear about how to take advantage of the employee's motivation.

12. Keep in mind that words are inadequate. Continuously seek to expand discussion with examples and specifics. Solicit feedback from employees as a check on meanings.

13. Continue negotiating the contract beyond the formal session. The first weeks of the contract are where actions give further clarity to verbiage. Managers and employees should treat this as a period of extended negotiation.

14. Align organizational parameters with contract requirements. Managers must be careful not to send inconsistent signals with systems, practices, or processes, not to mention with mission, vision, strategy, and culture. You do not want to argue that certain behaviors are critical and then direct your measurements and rewards in different directions.

15. Finally, legitimate renegotiation. Between the beginning and end of the contract, renegotiation may be necessary, especially in permanent white-water environments. Don't assume that one contract will last indefinitely.

Some Questions, Some Responses

Workforce diversity is the arena with which most people have the greatest familiarity; also, this is where many possess strong opinions and some concerns. I close this chapter with a brief consideration of three questions I hear frequently whenever workforce diversity is discussed.

Question 1: *How much longer will we need to concern ourselves with equal opportunity and affirmative action?*
Response: If you define equal opportunity as the state where all organizational participants are free from irrelevant barriers that block their development and contribution, if you agree that all such barriers are not necessarily the product of bias but also caused in part by limited ability to deal with complexity and diversity, and if you agree that we are just now placing diversity and complexity with respect to race and gender on the managerial agenda, then we can conclude that the necessary conditions for equal opportunity do not exist in most enterprises. At best, perhaps, we can say that in some organizations we have minimized biaslike behavior. We will need to continue our efforts with equal opportunity, affirmative action for equal opportunity, and affirmative action for equal rights.

I distinguish between affirmative action for equal opportunity and affirmative action for statistical parity or equal results. Affirmative action for equal opportunity advocates acting affirmatively to bring about equal opportunity until it (equal opportunity) becomes a natural process built into the very organizational fabric. On the other hand, affirmative action for equal results argues for acting affirmatively to bring about statistical parity until equal opportunity becomes a natural part of the enterprise's reality.

In reality, most corporations turn to affirmative action for equal results in desperation. Their managers essentially are admitting to not having been successful in bringing about equal opportunity, and for many this reality is frustrating and puzzling since they do not see themselves as racists or sexists. The analysis in this chapter suggests that the failure to realize equal opportunity may not be due to racism or sexism, but rather to managers' inability to deal with diversity and complexity.

The implication is that if managers wish to eliminate the need for affirmative action for equal opportunity and for affirmative action for equal results, they should move forward swiftly and vigorously with the Diversity Management process. As long as equal opportunity is not a reality, something comparable to both forms of affirmative action—regardless of what you call it—will be needed.

Question 2: *Aren't you making an erroneous, but critical, assumption that white males will give up power without a struggle?*

Response: Diversity Management does presume that the manager's priority is the best interests of the organization and not the maintenance of his power or that of his affinity group. Is this realistic?

Beyond any doubt, there are white-male managers who perceive any discussion of diversity as a threat to their power. Sometimes this is expressed as a question: "Why can't they [newcomers of all races] respect our way of doing business?" Sometimes it surfaces as resistance to the contention that economic environmental realities will force change. One manager suggested that white-male managers might be more receptive to change if it weren't forced on them, if they saw themselves as having options. So, some white-male managers do see this as a power struggle and resist accordingly.

However, other white-male managers readily see diversity as a managerial issue and not as a manifestation of a power struggle. These managers often have had some experience with defining diversity in arenas other than the workforce. They also tend to have little difficulty seeing it as a business issue. These managers will be one of the critical building blocks for change.

The power struggle perspective is a reality, but not the only one. White males have diverse views and understandings of diversity.

Question 3. *What do you do to assist white males who see diversity as a power-struggle issue?*

Response: You need to help them attain a conceptual understanding of Diversity Management and the reality that diversity means everyone. Without clarity on the differences among Diversity Management, affirmative action, and understanding differences, progress will be difficult.

Also, you should afford white-male managers an opportunity to talk about race and gender matters candidly and dispassionately. A dispassionate framework, at a minimum, would recognize causal factors of biaslike behavior other than racism or sexism. Such a framework would minimize the need for the white male to be in a defensive mode about the possibility of being labeled a racist or a sexist, and would foster open, problem-solving, productive dialogue.

I believe a core message of this chapter is that the Diversity Management process is such a dispassionate framework. I can easily see such a Diversity Management dialogue around these questions:

1. In the context of the Paradigm's action options, traditionally how have we as white males acted with respect to race and gender?
2. What have been the strengths and weaknesses of our approaches?
3. As we decide what approaches will be appropriate in the future, what factors should we take into account?
4. Given this analysis, what approaches would be most appropriate?
5. What action steps are required to facilitate adoption of these approaches?

If white males engage in this kind of dialogue, it would position them as critical forces for change for the benefit of organizational vitality.

Changing Times, Changing Terminology

Three methodologies—affirmative action, understanding differences, and Managing Diversity—are still in place and still valid approaches to workforce diversity. The components of these three correspond to the eight action options of the Diversity Paradigm. That is to say, when what you're dealing with is a diversity concern that relates to the workforce, you have—using the traditional terminology that most people are familiar with—three options; they are the same as the eight options of the Diversity Paradigm, which is new vocabulary to most people. In other words, when diversity in the workforce is your concern, you have three ways to go: affirmative action, understanding differences, and Managing Diversity. Collectively, they correspond to eight action options of the Diversity Paradigm. Thus, Managing Diversity is *one* part of Diversity Management, the part specifically targeted at the workforce. To summarize:

- *Diversity Management* is a process for addressing diversity in all of its dimensions, *including* the workforce, through the eight action options of the Diversity Paradigm.
- *Managing Diversity* is a process for addressing workforce diversity through a single vehicle: mutual adaptation.

Exhibit 5-1 describes in more detail the relationship of these three processes.

The Diversity Learning Curve

I have spent many years as an educator, and I am continually in awe of the capacity of the human brain to expand to receive new ideas. It's as if a part of our mind opens up to take in a

Exhibit 5-1. Diversity in the workforce: old and new terminology.

Affirmative Action	*Understanding Differences*	*Managing Diversity*
• Include/exclude • Deny • Isolate (segregate) • Suppress • Assimilate	• Tolerate • Build relationships	• Foster mutual adaptation

new thought and then, as we fully assimilate that new concept, it opens up even wider, to accommodate even greater understanding.

We can observe that process at work with the concepts of diversity. The most visible form of diversity that most of us have experienced is diversity among people; it has also been the most difficult, when it surfaces in the context of racism and sexism. To alleviate the tension that comes with these "isms," affirmative action and then understanding differences were developed.

Then, to enable all in the workforce to do their best work (not just women and racial minorities), I developed the idea that came to be called Managing Diversity.

And now we are learning a much broader philosophy that I have named Diversity Management, which can be applied to all areas of business concern, including but not limited to the workforce.

There is a process of mental evolution at work here. Moving away from a mindset based on the familiar "isms" to the more strategic concept of Managing Diversity is one phase; moving on from there to the more comprehensive concept of Diversity Management is yet another phase.

In Part Two you will read the experiences of several forward-thinking organizations that are working with diversity issues. The leaders of these organizations have moved beyond race and gender in their thinking, and now use the tool of Managing Diversity to focus their activities. But an amazing thing happens: The more they work with diversity, the broader their thinking becomes. For these leaders, diversity is beginning to mean much more than people diversity.

As their understanding of diversity expands, their tool for addressing diversity must also expand. They have gone from using affirmative action and understanding differences, to Managing Diversity; now they are ready to learn a new tool, the Diversity Paradigm. Language comes last. Even though most call their current efforts Managing Diversity, they are actually incorporating the precepts of Diversity Management process. They may not yet use the term, but they are in fact moving toward Diversity Management.

Part Two
Diversity at Work

6

There Is Life Beyond Work: Diversity of Lifestyle Concerns

Case Study: BellSouth Corporation

Up until very recently, issues related to employees' families and lifestyles were relegated to the personnel department—if they were considered at all.[1] Historically, these concerns have been designated "personal and private,"[2] and expected to be addressed before 8 A.M. and after 5 P.M. Whatever problems people had at home, they were expected to leave at home. Once at work, they were expected to fit into organizational norms without protest, and employees went along.[3]

Many organizational environments continue to encourage that kind of unquestioning assimilation, but employees no longer automatically go along. They are bringing their family concerns to work with them, and employers are forced to pay attention. They must pay attention because of three undeniable trends: Demographics of the workforce are changing, employee attitudes toward work are changing, and related tension is growing.

Consider just two statistics: It is projected that women will make up 48 percent of the workforce by the year 2005.[4]

Already, 60 percent of all employees have child- or elder-care responsibilities.[5] The implications of these statistics are enormous. Managers must, at a minimum, create an environment that allows women to reach their full potential in pursuit of organizational objectives. But they must also create an environment that facilitates the career success of (1) men, whose family-related responsibilities increase when their partners enter the workforce, of (2) single parents of both genders, and of (3) employees who participate in any number of traditional and nontraditional family constellations.

Indeed, society's definition of what constitutes *family* is evolving so thoroughly that business terminology in this area is changing too. As I move through corporations, I increasingly hear the broader term *lifestyle* as the umbrella name for all these issues, replacing *work/family*, with its connotation of having to balance or choose between the two. Thus corporations must be prepared to hear about, and respond to, all manner of employees' lifestyle concerns.

Increasingly, they must also accommodate a growing change in attitudes toward work. The Organization Man of the 1950s, who gave his all to the company, has retired; his offspring now work for the company, and they have different priorities. They care passionately about doing a good job, but they also want to devote time to family and personal goals. They are searching for a balance.[6]

One senior executive who has moved several times in her career, reported, "I gave up virtually everything to support what I was doing on the job. . . . in effect, I married the company."[7] She's not certain that she has made the right choice. Her experience is increasingly common. Human resources professionals report seeing numerous career-oriented employees who feel that the commitment and sacrifice that helped them get ahead in their careers has left them far behind in the other arenas of their lives.[8]

The difficulty is that corporations have been slow to acknowledge that lifestyle issues have a legitimate place on the managerial agenda. Their corporate culture, which derives from a different era, meshes poorly with today's changing workforce demographics and changing attitudes toward work and family. A gap is thus growing between the values and demands of today's workforce and the nature and expectations of America's traditional corporate cultures, and the immediate consequence of that gap is diversity tension.

This tension gets expressed in continuing debates about glass ceilings, child care, elder care, dual-career families, and work/lifestyle balance. It gets expressed in the backlash that emerges when one group perceives another as receiving preferential treatment. The negative economic consequences of this kind of tension may finally force companies to pay attention.

Managing the Changing Workplace

The basic principles of Diversity Management provide a framework to help us understand the profound changes taking place in the workforce, and also can help us move toward finding a solution.

Let us begin by seeing that what we are dealing with here is another type of diversity mixture. In the old corporation, managers assumed that all employees were homogeneous with respect to lifestyle parameters (because any specific problems were kept separate from work). In the new corporation, managers must learn to cope with multiple lifestyle variables, which are similar in some respects and different in other respects—in other words, a classic diversity mix. Making that adjustment is a massive challenge, fraught with complexity and risk. What we know about Diversity Management can be brought to bear on this challenge.

Assimilation

Old-style managers still rely on assimilation to bring about the kind of relationships between the individual and the or-

ganization that they consider desirable. They have little tolerance for deviations from the prevailing norm, and they have
difficulty accepting lifestyle diversity.

Assimilation-oriented managers often are unaware of Diversity Management's options and the reality that they have
choices. Further, it is not clear that they would use alternatives even if they knew of them. They may be ideologically
bound to the status quo, or they may lack the flexibility required to explore options. Least likely to embrace alternatives
are "institutional" managers (see Chapter 3) who have seen
the status quo produce great results.

Isolation

Managers in some companies isolate lifestyle concerns from
diversity efforts, reserving the word *diversity* for minority issues. *Work/family* becomes synonymous with women's issues.

This is understandable. They may be trying to ensure
that the topic receives sufficient attention and/or to avoid the
baggage associated with minority issues and affirmative action. On the other hand, this kind of separation may reflect
inability to think about several issues at one time. To facilitate
matters (to minimize the amount of diversity and complexity), they isolate the issues and focus on each set in turn. Managers are often supported in this by lifestyle advocates eager
to ensure that their particular issue attracts the manager's attention.

Yet there are shortcomings to this approach. Sustainable
progress with lifestyle concerns requires the same capability
to accept, understand, and address diversity as does progress
with minority issues. Both issues manifest the generic dynamics of diversity. Keeping them separate encourages
"what-have-you-done-for-*me*-lately?" rivalries between the
two camps and creates dysfunctional divisiveness. It's not uncommon, for example, to hear minority advocates complain
that efforts aimed at work/family (women's) concerns are
taken more seriously than those devoted to minority issues.

Keeping the efforts separate has an additional disadvantage. It results in lost opportunities to gain synergy through Diversity Management. If managers understood the dynamics undergirding the Diversity Management framework, they could expand their diversity and complexity capabilities and devise interventions that simultaneously advanced progress with diversity and lifestyle. This would prevent costly and sometimes counterproductive duplication of efforts.

Isolation is widespread. Diversity efforts are not just isolated by groups but also isolated from mainstream systems. Lifestyle efforts, in particular, have been characterized primarily by programs. Isolating the company's official response into a program allows organizations to address the issue without disturbing mainstream practices and systems.

Isolation through programs often makes sense. When they first perceive diversity tension related to lifestyle issues, managers are not certain what to think. Is this a fad? How widespread are concerns about the issue? Just what do these people want? If the tension persists, and if efforts to assimilate, ignore (exclude), deny, and suppress don't work, an option is to create some kind of program. It provides some relief to the advocates, avoids disturbing the status quo significantly, and gives managers time to gain further understanding and to plan actions.

Yet program interventions alone—without cultural and system changes and mindset shifts—will produce limited progress. This has been the case with racial workforce issues and is proving to be true for lifestyle issues as well.

Tension Between Groups

An additional problem is that often corporations define lifestyle issues very narrowly. This narrowness becomes another form of isolation and the root of significant tension between employee groups.

Until recently, lifestyle issues were synonymous with women's issues. Even now, elder and child care dominate the lifestyle arena. However, nearly two thirds of U.S. workers do not have children under eighteen, and many employees have other, unaddressed lifestyle concerns. Those who are inconvenienced by efforts to address elder- and child-care issues are beginning to complain.[9]

Their list of grievances is long. Childless workers complain that they're expected to work longer hours, forfeit more weekends, and be transferred more often. While at work, they frequently answer phones and absorb extra work to cover for parents who arrive late or leave early to deliver or retrieve children. Many also report that benefit packages favor families with children.

A more inclusive approach would minimize such resentments. Some companies are experimenting with such an approach. A *Wall Street Journal* report, for example, described one company that offers flextime to all employees, and another that gives a $300 annual credit to childless employees, who generate lower medical insurance costs. They can use the credit to buy up to three days of extra vacation.[10]

Empowerment

Broadening the definition of lifestyle diversity, recognizing the breadth of possible variations, and addressing the multiple possibilities requires a Diversity Management ability. This, in turn, requires an adequate management ability as a base. Our research in corporations suggests that this cannot be assumed.

Many executives do not require managers to empower their employees, despite senior management rhetoric and training program prescriptions. Nonempowerment managers (see Chapter 4) are less motivated to maximize the utilization of people with different lifestyle patterns. My observations suggest that even if motivated, these managers are unlikely to know how to modify culture and systems to bring about the desired environment. The magnitude of the task and the necessity for vision intimidate managers who are trained to focus on short-term performance goals and objectives and are rewarded for doing so.

Part of the problem is a failure to see employees as strategic. Managers may care deeply about their employees' welfare, desire to be fair, and share the benefits of success. Yet few managers see people as critical to maintaining competitive enterprises. Instead, they tend to think the crucial factors are technology, product innovation, and quality, and only minimally connect these factors to the efforts of people. Yet technology is not like oil coming from the ground; it comes from technologically capable *people*. This inability to see people as strategic allows managers to place a low priority on empowering people in general, and an even lower priority on empowering people who are different with respect to lifestyle.

Cultural Change

Think of your organization as a tree. The roots of that tree are the fundamental assumptions that uphold the tree: in other words, the company's culture. The branches of the tree are the visible activities as the company goes about its business.[11] Program-type remedies regarding lifestyle issues call for flexibility in organizational practices—that is, for changes in the branches. But until the roots (the culture) are also modified, those changes in practice will be short-lived.

Once again, the Diversity Management process can help us understand why this is so. Management's limited ability to accept, understand, and address diversity and complexity effectively hampers their ability to address simultaneously changes in roots and branches. Roots are conceptual; branches are more concrete. Roots are unseen and sometimes unacknowledged; branches are more visible. Finally, roots take longer than branches to change. Managers, who have far more experience with branch than with root change, tend to focus on branches rather than address both roots and branches at once.

Difficulty with diversity and complexity hampers *any* change where root modifications are required, especially if exclusion, denial, or suppression are used to minimize diversity tension.

How Diversity Management Can Help

Without Diversity Management, managers wrestling with lifestyle concerns tend to think win or lose, all or nothing. Diversity Management allows managers and employees to focus effectively—like a wide-angle camera lens—on more than one thing at a time. This expansion of focus can free managers to explore a broader range of possibility and an even greater variety of combinations. It also allows for a diverse approach, using different options to address different aspects of an issue, as well as a dynamic approach where selections of options might change over time. Equally important, it offers a framework for individual employees struggling to find an appropriate balance between work and personal life.

The Managerial Perspective

Managers have two diversity mixtures to address. The first is the various lifestyle parameters that employees bring to the work site. Relevant questions include: How will I ever accommodate all of these differences? How serious are employees about pressing for action about their lifestyle issues? Can I simply cling to the status quo and count on people to adjust? What do I want to signal to employees regarding my position on lifestyle matters?

The Diversity Paradigm provides a framework for thinking through this complexity:

Include/exclude: Legal and political realities make it
                            difficult to exclude or include peo-

ple solely because of their lifestyle parameters. But managers do have a limited ability to minimize lifestyle diversity through inclusion or exclusion, and may seek to draw on this alternative and its decreasing potential.

Deny:

By refusing to recognize lifestyle diversity, managers can simplify their lives and act as if everyone were the same. As employees become more adamant in demanding consideration of their differences, managers using this option risk losing touch with reality.

Isolate:

Here, the manager breaks the mixture down and isolates the different groupings. On one hand, this simplifies his task. He can continue the status quo where appropriate and move to sequentially address the needs of the remaining groups. On the other hand, this option brings its own problems and tensions, as the unattended groups develop a "what have you done for me lately?" attitude. Before he can fully institutionalize his response to, say, the dual-career group, single parents begin to clamor for attention. By the time he makes his rounds, the limited progress with the first groupings comes under duress, and he starts the cycle again. This makes for a lot of activity and effort, but little *sustainable* progress.

Suppress:

Here the manager encourages groups to suppress their differences, to leave them at the organization's door. She does not want to hear about employees' lifestyle problems. Suppression can simplify the manager's challenge if employees are willing to go along. However, as employees become more comfortable with their differences, they are more likely to resist this option.

Assimilate:

In this option the manager identifies the desired set of lifestyle parameters and encourages employees to conform. Lifestyle prescriptions might, for example, dictate the desired characteristics of spouses, the timing and number of children, and the appropriate management of elder-care issues. Many readers will find these prescriptions objectionable, but just a few years ago, such assimilation dictates were common.

Tolerate:

The manager begrudgingly acknowledges the reality and legitimacy of nontraditional lifestyle parameters, but he never warmly or intimately engages the groups that are different. There may be rhetoric about becoming enlightened corporations, but members of the different groups remain painfully aware of their tolerated status.

Build relationships:

The manager seeks to accept and understand each lifestyle grouping.

She learns about each's concerns and needs and earns a reputation as being sensitive to lifestyle issues. But no real change takes place in the organization's ability to address lifestyle complexities. Relationship building can simply foster understanding and good feelings, or it can set the stage for mutual adaptation.

Foster mutual adaptation: The manager understands that lifestyle diversity/complexity will be an enduring reality for the foreseeable future, and acknowledges that individual and organization mindsets will have to shift. She focuses actively on the mixture and on the development of mindsets and practices reflecting the diversity and complexity. She gives attention to changing managers', employees', and organization parameters as well.

Managers who decide to move forward with diversity create another diversity mixture as well: the mix of change efforts in the lifestyle arena on the one hand and efforts in other arenas on the other. In addressing this mixture, the relevant questions include: How should lifestyle efforts relate to other change thrusts? Where should they be housed? Should lifestyle activities be integrated with others, or set up as a separate program? Is there a need for officer oversight and involvement? Should lifestyle results in this area be incorporated into the financial rewards process?

The Diversity Management process can help managers sort out these complexities. As an exercise, you might find it revealing to think through applying the Paradigm to this mixture.

Employee Perspectives

The employee's role is critical if organizations are to succeed in addressing the lifestyle issue. Like their managers, employees must address a diversity mix, but theirs is different: the collective mix of life activities.

All individuals have a set of activities around which they build their lives. Some activities are included by choice, others by necessity. Work falls under the second category for the majority of people. Several questions are pertinent to the lifestyle mix: How should I allocate my time among the activities? What, if any, priorities should I have? How do I resolve conflicting demands among the activities? How do I minimize stress as I deal with conflicting activity demands? How do I enhance my capacity to do all I would like to do?

Here, too, the Diversity Paradigm can provide a framework for thinking through these questions:

Include/exclude:	The include/exclude options are basic to each individual's efforts to manage his diversity mixture of life activities. Individuals may add to their mixture because they either have no choice or have unfilled needs. They may exclude activities because these activities don't meet their existing needs or because they wish to simplify their lives. Examples of exclusion are deciding to stay at home after having a baby or postponing expanding a family to leave resources for current activities.
Deny:	Here the individual denies the magnitude of the complexity and diversity of her mixture and does her best to fulfill the requirements

of each activity. Denial may be achieved by framing the conflicts and complexity as aspects of day-to-day living experienced by everyone or as something that "hard work" can overcome.

Isolate: The employee deals with the diversity and complexity of life's activities through rigid isolation. Work is work; family time is family time; play time is a period that cannot be violated. This segregation of activity and time can minimize complexity and conflicting demands only if the person has control of her activities. As organizations downsize and require more work from remaining employees, the employee's "control" is often compromised.

Suppress: The employee recognizes complexities and conflicting demands but suppresses them, either because he is unable to cope with them cognitively or because he is not ready to make decisions about his activities. Suppression removes these factors from the individual's awareness.

Assimilate: In this option the person minimizes complexity and stress by assimilating the activities. At one extreme, work becomes the context for everything (often the case in "company towns"); at the other extreme, family becomes the context for everything. Where work is the defining reality, the individual looks to the work setting to fulfill as many needs as possible; where family is the defining context, this unit becomes the center of most life activities.

Tolerate: Here the individual has a dominant set of activities, but he includes and recognizes others and acknowledges the consequent complexities and conflicts. He perceives himself as juggling work and family, but readily admits that some of the juggled "balls" don't get as much attention as they need. Representative here is the father who, knowing work is dominant and conflicting with other activities, attempts to be available for his family on special occasions but cannot bring about the shifts in time allocations that would allow him to do so regularly. This individual often has a partner who relies on toleration, perhaps one whose major focus is on family, but who also works part-time and is supportive of her partner's choices.

Build relationships: Employees who use this option intimately explore the complexity dimensions and alternatives for coping. They look at interrelationships among their activities and the possibilities for including them all without undue stress. They have a sense of where there might be overlaps and how they might leverage these. They also have a sense of what their priorities should be. They, like individuals who choose toleration, may have a sense of juggling life activities, but they do so with more success. These people may be said to have a *balanced* life.

Foster mutual adaptation: This employee, often after an intense exploration in "building relationships," decides to do what's necessary to bring about the balancing *and* integrating of life's activities into a meaningful and fulfilling whole. This person can be said to have an *integrated* life—one that allows for balance with meaning.

This process of balancing and integrating life activities is just beginning to receive attention. The Diversity Management process offers a context for this introspection.

Diversity Management, Balance, and Integration

In the preceding section, I alluded to individuals who develop a balanced life and an integrated life, with the implication that there is some distinction between the two. What is the difference? People who achieve a balanced life have all the appropriate experiences in their life—work, family, recreation, volunteer activities, etc.—and allocate the proper time for each. In an integrated life, the desired components are not simply present but are interrelated and integrated appropriately into a broader context that gives meaning to the whole and makes the sum greater than the parts.

People who live *balanced lives* focus on maintaining the balance, not on any one component or even on the whole. Achieving a balanced life may be sufficient for many individuals. But it carries with it an implicit concern for managers:

The balanced life prohibits all-consuming dedication to work at a time when permanent white-water environments more than ever demand commitment.

Individuals who live *integrated lives* act within an overarching theme. This theme connects the diverse and often conflicting roles they assume, providing these roles and life in general with a significance and meaning that can't be explained by examining the individual parts. Work, for example, becomes more than work. It becomes a vehicle for the pursuit of a broader meaning.

The decision whether to strive for balance *and* integration is the intrapersonal lifestyle issue with which all of us must make our peace. When accepted, the personal, individual diversity challenge calls for including the "right" experiences and developing an integrating life theme that gives meaning to life and relates the parts. Doing so requires an ability to include and integrate simultaneously—that is, to accept, understand, and address diversity appropriately.

What is the role of the manager in all this? Managers are not responsible for seeing that their employees achieve balanced, integrated lives. Only individuals can seek and attain this ideal. But managers can foster this process by modeling it within the organization. One way to do this is to create and articulate what have been termed *superordinate goals*—"the goals above all others."[12] Superordinate goals provide the glue that holds an organization's structure, strategies, systems, style, staff, and skills together. In effect, they give meaning to an organization's work.

In his 1955 *Harvard Business Review* classic, " 'Skyhooks' With Special Implications for Monday through Friday," O. A. Ohmann calls these superordinate goals "skyhooks,"[13] something the individual "can believe in and trust and that gives meaning to his activities." Skyhooks are broad, big-picture propositions that pull people individually and collectively to a higher calling. They can, for example, rationalize an individual's work, volunteer activities, recreation, religious efforts, and approach to parenting; similarly, they can provide the focus for the evolution of a corporation. Examples include "We seek to keep America strong" and "We seek to serve humankind."

People vary as to what superordinate goals they can embrace. As a result, the more diverse the workforce, the more challenging it becomes to foster skyhooking. Ohmann links the ability to do so to the ability of the manager:

> . . . in a managerial society, this brings us back to the quality of the administrator. He interprets or crystallizes. He sets the climate within which these values either *do* or *do not* become working realities. He must define the goals and purposes of his group in larger and more meaningful perspective. He integrates the smaller, selfish goals of individuals into larger, more social and spiritual objectives for the group. He provides the vision without which the people perish. Conflicts are resolved by relating the immediate to the long-range and more enduring values. In fact, we might say this *integrative function* is the core of the administrator's contribution.[14]

Managers perform this integrative function as part of their *leadership* role. By clarifying mission, vision, and strategy and by building a supportive culture, they offer skyhooks that associates may use or reject. Managers cannot force or require skyhooking; they can only encourage.

Why is skyhooking important? Because it facilitates the commitment required in permanent white water. Committed employees don't mimic the Organization Man; instead, they make connections between the meanings embedded in the organization and those around which their life is grounded. Work becomes an extension of life. This allows individuals to commit—to bring all they can to the table (work) for a period of time without sacrificing the opportunity for a balanced life.

Committed individuals don't need to be "micromanaged." Whether in the office, at home, or in the field, they are fully engaged. The ideal in the midst of white-water environments is committed workers who have skyhooked and are leading balanced *and* integrated lives.

In the language of the Diversity Paradigm, skyhooking facilitates mutual adaptation by helping people clarify the ways in which they can integrate work into their larger life themes. This allows them to achieve cohesiveness and synergy without unnecessarily compromising the integrity of each life activity. As a result, diversity tension related to work/family concerns is minimized—a benefit to both individuals and their organizations.

The BellSouth Story*

BellSouth recognizes the challenges that each employee faces as work place demands, career objectives, family needs and personal goals compete for time and attention. The corporation is committed to helping employees identify and use effective resources to meet these challenges. These efforts promote quality service for our customers and a competitive edge in the marketplace by enhancing the contribution of BellSouth's diverse employees.

—Roy Howard, former Senior Vice President,
Corporate Human Resources, BellSouth Corporation

This statement by Roy Howard captures the spirit of the BellSouth Corporation's work/family efforts. These activities are aimed at helping employees attain a balance between work and personal life. While many options have been sanctioned and put in place by the corporation, managers have had significant discretion in how these options evolve.

Initial concerns with work/family issues date back to

*This case is based on reviews of reports and other materials made available by BellSouth.

1990, when then corporate vice chairman Duane Ackerman empowered a committee called The Work and Personal Life Team to identify emerging critical issues in the lifestyle arena. This committee conducted a survey and used a variety of other resources to gather data. These data, which identified demographic trends and employee stress as major issues, provided the motivation for addressing work/family issues—later called work/personal life issues.

Demographic Trends

The committee identified several demographic shifts that made attention to personal issues seem important. Most of the projected workforce changes concerned the supply of human resources.

The average age of BellSouth's workforce has increased more rapidly than that of the population at large, as a result of the company's history of long-term employment and limited growth opportunities for regulated companies. Management realized that recruitment will become critical in the near future as current employees reach retirement age. They also realized that available recruits will differ significantly from the employees now in place, both in numbers of qualified applicants and in characteristics of gender, race, ethnicity, and lifestyle. The question quickly became, is BellSouth prepared to attract and empower the cream of the available crop?

Stress Trends

The committee buttressed its argument with data that indicated that the company's approach to workforce issues, which had been developed within traditional work/family parameters, was no longer working well. A stress audit of more than 3,000 BellSouth employees indicated that a significant number of them were experiencing considerable stress, and that family, personal, and work challenges were major causes.

Family-related stresses included child- and elder-care problems, relocation difficulties, and financial concerns.

Personal stressors included life balance, personal development, aging concerns, and mental and physical health issues. Work-related stressors included company/employee relations; manager/employee relations; implementing of work teams; employee development; issues around compensation, advancement, and recognition; unclear job responsibilities; and pressure to excel.

Using national workplace stress data, the committee estimated that this stress was costly for BellSouth. Information specific to BellSouth confirmed the conclusion. Stress-related illnesses (psychoses, depressive neuroses, alcohol/drug abuse or dependency, neuroses, and depression) constituted five of the company's top ten diagnostic groups for hospital services. Two others—coronary bypass and back problems, both closely linked to stress—accounted for significant benefit payments. Further, sixteen of the twenty-five drugs most frequently dispensed to BellSouth employees were for treatment of stress-related illnesses.

The committee believed that work, the third major source of stress, would stay dynamic and would continue to be characterized by significant change. Employees were likely to have ongoing and even increased difficulty in balancing work and personal life. Committee members believed that helping employees to cope with family and personal issues not only would reduce the overall level of stress but would create a better environment for further workplace change. In the Diversity Paradigm's language, committee members believed that individuals already experiencing diversity tension with respect to personal, family, and work issues would encounter even more stress as planned workplace modifications went forward. This increased tension could result in increased stress-related costs and decreased ability to implement change plans.

Action

Committee members responded to their findings by making several recommendations with respect to benefits, practices, work flexibility arrangements, and stress management. Equally important, the committee's research and resulting recommendations generated significant action.

One outcome of this activity is that substantial unpaid leaves of absence are available, as are personal and dependent-care leaves. Some work groups are experimenting with flexible work arrangements such as part-time jobs, flexible scheduling, and four-day workweeks. Stress management is taught in brown-bag lunch seminars and articles in BellSouth publications. All programs and benefits related to work/personal life have been summarized in a brochure entitled "Your Life and Work: A Shared Responsibility," which details offerings available to employees.

BellSouth has made innovative use of selected features such as sabbatical leaves and flextime to facilitate temporary downsizing. Corporate Human Resources staff have assembled a variety of tools to help managers in making decisions regarding these options. These managers use their discretion to determine the extent to which the options are allowed.

Moving Toward a Strategic Approach

BellSouth initially responded to the work/personal life arena largely by developing programs. This is isolation. These programs have not been widely or uniformly used, although some high-profile success stories exist. The company's initial experience has provided a solid foundation for further progress.

A positive benefit of the initial isolation option has been that the corporation has had time to become more familiar with work/personal life issues, yielding a greater appreciation of the importance of work/personal life as a business issue. In addition, a growing understanding is evolving that effective, sustainable implementation will require a "way of life" change for BellSouth—in other words, mutual adaptation. Toward this end, committee members have been evolving a comprehensive framework that connects work/personal life to managerial processes and the bottom line.

The Work and Personal Life Team is seeking to create conditions favorable to mutual adaptation by positioning work/personal life as a diversity issue and establishing diversity as a strategic issue.

In constructing the argument for the diversity framework, team members noted projected demographic shifts in race and gender, the growing diversity of the company's marketplace (including its international operations), the increasing diversity of employees' changing expectations, shifting family patterns among employees, and the tightening labor markets served by BellSouth.

The team also reported the results of a survey indicating that employees believed that diversity was important to them but felt that BellSouth was not doing a good job in dealing with it. Fewer than half of the respondents knew of BellSouth's programs addressing work, family, and personal issues. In addition, 45 percent felt that few or none of the policies and practices that BellSouth implements are sensitive to their lives outside of work.

The Work and Personal Life Team offered recommendations designed to ensure that work/personal life interventions previously implemented continue in force. Team members asked that flexible work arrangements become an essential element of course development for managers and supervisors; that course development for managers and supervisors include methodology for appraising work in situations where the individual employee is not working on-site; that benefit plans continue to recognize and support individuality; and that equivalent head count be substituted for head count as a methodology and convention in budgeting, payroll activity, and work-group sizing decisions. They also asked

that BellSouth continue to help employees identify and support the use of effective resources that help individuals to balance work and personal life.

Some Lessons

BellSouth is stepping out significantly with work/personal
life issues. The efforts retain a "program" feel, but this is a
short-term stage. The company is moving to broaden work/
personal life to include concerns about life balance, by inter-
twining special programs in this area into systems that serve
all employees. It continues to focus on the strategic significance of work/personal life issues, and on connections of this
arena to other initiatives. *The company is moving toward mutual
adaptation to preserve competitiveness.*

From their experiences, we can draw four critical lessons.

1. The Diversity Paradigm can be a useful managerial
tool for diagnosing, understanding, and action planning in
lifestyle issues. Diversity Management offers insights as to
why lifestyle has become a managerial issue now and why
progress in the area has been limited. It also offers implications for next steps.

2. The Diversity Paradigm can help managers conceptualize and address the challenges created by two conflicting
trends: uncertain complex environments that call for intense
employee engagement and commitment, and the multiple
loyalties (demands) created as employees increasingly seek
balance in the lifestyle arena.

3. The Diversity Paradigm provides the change agent
with a useful perspective about programs. Frequently, people
advocating change say, "Don't throw a program at this
issue." Their perspective is understandable. Programs are
often used as Band-Aids and don't lead to meaningful
change. But the paradigm suggests that programs *can* help
managers to clarify their understanding of the issue before

moving to formulate realistic action plans for systemic change. When used for this purpose, programs become possible foundations for change.

4. Individual facility with the Diversity Paradigm on the part of managers and employees can enable its use interpersonally and organizationally. The mindset shifts that occur when managers and associates use the Diversity Paradigm as a common conceptual framework from which to address lifestyle issues can benefit both individuals and their organizations. More important, however, is that the nature of this framework encourages a broader perspective and a greater understanding of the interdependency of people and their organizations.

7

Breaking Out of Silos: Diversity of Functions
Case Study: Hallmark Cards

Organizations usually evolve from the simple to the complex. Most businesses move through a fairly standard growth pattern. They start out with a single product or category of product, or a single service. If they do not do well with that first product, they go out of business. If they prosper, they almost invariably expand into other products, other territories, and/or other lines of business. As the company's product mix becomes more complex, so does its structure. Continued success creates the need for even more new developments. Thus prosperity and complexity move forward hand in hand.

At some point, the growth curve produces an unmanageable amount of complexity. Managers and employees are asked to fulfill too many demands, process too much data, and make too many decisions. They first feel overwhelmed, then angry and paralyzed.

It's both impractical and unreasonable to hold employees responsible for multiple tasks that exceed their complexity capabilities. The person who did a fine job scheduling seasonal workers when the company had just two product lines for one market will hit overload when asked to schedule workers in twelve different specialties for three hundred products; ask that same person to set up new manufacturing facilities offshore, and you risk disaster.

At that point, the usual tactic that organizations have employed is some measure of specialization.

Specialization

Specialization involves organizing the structure of the company around tasks, and grouping similar tasks into one unit (department, division, work team, whatever). By congregating together the activities related to one task or several similar tasks, organizations hope to simplify, achieve efficiency, and maximize individual contributions.

Specialization tends to have a homogenizing effect on the work unit. This homogenization facilitates effectiveness, economies of scale and of learning, flow of information, and problem solving. It also allows easier meshing of accountabilities and responsibilities. Managers responsible for a task are more easily held accountable in task-centered structures. Specialization is a vehicle for minimizing complexity.

Taken to its ultimate with respect to functions, specialization gives rise to units that are largely self-contained. Sometimes referred to as silos or stovepipes, these units can develop thick walls that foster and protect appropriate internal dynamics but hamper communications among the functions.

We usually think of these specialized units in terms of the differences in their task, or function. But things are not quite so simple. They differ with respect to culture (basic assumptions), degree of formality, time orientation, and the nature of interpersonal relationships among employees as well.[1]

A classic example is the difference between Manufacturing on the one hand and Research and Development on the other. In addition to the task differences—producing a product versus conducting research and developing new products or refining existing ones—these units are likely to differ in other significant ways:

1. *Hierarchy:* high formality in Manufacturing versus low formality in Research
2. *Time orientation:* short-term in Manufacturing versus long-term in Research
3. *Interpersonal relationships:* high formality in Manufacturing versus low formality in Research[2]

These parameters can result in two very different operations.

From a specialization perspective, the units work best when they are completely self-contained and interact with other units only in minimal, predictable ways. That promotes organizational proficiency and minimizes diversity tension. The flip side of this is that the more successful they are at becoming independent, the more difficulty they will have collaborating with other units.

As long as the external environment remains stable, this is not a problem. The status quo can profitably continue. But if changes in the organization's environment compromise the existing success formulas, specialization loses its positive character. The threat to viability makes all departments interdependent in the search for new ways to thrive.

Efforts at interdependence usually don't go smoothly. When units that have long been dissimilar and seen their independence as a source of pride are asked to collaborate in spite of their differences and segregated states, tension can become quite intense. Since energy spent on tension is wasted energy, serious productivity gaps result. For example:

> One divisional president saw relations among his functions grow so strained and heated that essential cooperation could not occur. At one session, he stood up and literally shouted: "People, the enemy is not inside! We are not the enemy! The enemy is outside."

Dysfunctional tension of this sort has the potential to generate continuous organizational problems.

Finding the Balance

The challenge is to achieve the necessary degree of interaction between units while preserving an appropriate level of separateness—to find the balance between independence and collaboration.

Sometimes this can be accomplished by using a third party (either an individual or a department) to integrate the work of two units.[3] This integrating process goes on outside the units, while they continue their usual work independent of each other. In other cases, the integration between units requires breaking through the segregated walls and pushing each independent unit to make changes so that collaboration is possible.[4]

Expressed in the terminology of the Diversity Paradigm, keeping work units independent to capitalize on the efficiencies that this permits is *isolation;* pushing units to modify their processes to facilitate the breaking down of walls in order to make collaboration possible is *mutual adaptation.* Finding a balance between these two approaches is itself a diversity challenge.

Individuals and Departments as Integrators[5]

Using specific individuals as integrators is not new. Professional services firms have been doing it for quite some time: They call the integrating person "project manager." Traditionally, project managers have had to balance two opposing forces: giving the separate functions all the independence they need to do their best work, while simultaneously promoting the unity of effort needed to fulfill the project.

Where this unity is relatively easy to achieve, project management can be an informal, part-time role, filled by a person who has other responsibilities in the firm. Through personal influence, that person rallies resources from various functions on behalf of the project. This informal system works best in a relatively stable, predictable task environment, and it usually has only minimal effect on the segregated walls of the functional silos.

A variation on this approach is to designate temporary teams to manage the project and provide the integration mechanism. These teams are composed of individuals from the various functions involved in the project, and a team or project leader. At any given time, an individual might serve as project leader on one team and as a member on another. While still informal, this option permits greater penetration of silos. It also requires a greater comfort with diversity and complexity than some functional participants have.

This rotating arrangement can continue indefinitely as long as the functions remain relatively independent and technologies change slowly and predictably. However, if tasks or environments change to the extent that success formulas are threatened, the project leader's role must be enhanced.

Integration between functions can be provided by departments as well. Precedents exist in business: a scheduling department that works between sales and manufacturing, or an applied research department that converts the basic research of R&D into products. How they are set up and operated is closely related to external environmental realities.

Sometimes these departments operate as self-contained units; they receive information from one function and pass it to another. The separation between functions is maintained.

When the environment is stable and clear, this one-way coordination can work well. But when the environment is turbulent and change is occurring rapidly, the interaction between functions becomes more complex.[6] In this situation, the integrating department must see that information moves in multiple directions simultaneously. This can involve creating cross-functional teams and designating specific people from various functions as liaisons to supplement the integrating department's efforts and facilitate collaboration.

If neither of these approaches—using individuals or departments to provide the necessary integration between functions—is sufficient, organizations may need to turn to more-formalized solutions. Two common approaches are the matrix organization and full-blown reengineering.

The Matrix Organization

The matrix, a natural evolutionary result of strained project/product manager structures, overlays a product management structure on a functional structure. As such, it gives managers great flexibility in maintaining balance between product/project perspectives and perspectives required to foster functional effectiveness and efficiency. The matrix fits most appropriately where there is a high need to be responsive to two segments—for example, external customers and functional technologies.[7]

Without doubt, implementing the matrix structure presents challenges. Senior management must be able to be firm and inflexible about creating conditions that will allow a flexible organization to thrive, and to be comfortable with the mixed signals implicit in this behavior.[8] Mid-level managers, both functional and project, must be able to adjust to changed roles.[9] Functional managers often feel the matrix diminishes their standing. Project managers find themselves choosing continually between using the formal authority of their position or the informal levers of their interpersonal skills. Employees at nearly all levels must juggle the sometimes contradictory demands of two bosses.[10]

For all these reasons, working within a matrix structure requires mental flexibility. Managers cannot concentrate on just one role or process. This means that, at bottom, implementing a matrix is a diversity challenge. It involves fostering a mindset that can embrace the complexity of a diversity mixture of two bosses. Some people are simply unable to do this. It is not surprising, therefore, that many managers resist the matrix or report negative experiences of tension, conflict, and confusion.

Can the matrix structure work? At the moment, the jury is still out. We do know, however, that if the environmental realities that gave rise to the matrix persist, organizations will have to do something to enhance employees' ability to deal with complexity. Alternately, they must find some method. One is reengineering.

Reengineering

Formally defined, *reengineering* is "the fundamental rethinking and radical design of business processes to achieve dramatic improvements in critical, contemporary measures of performance, such as cost, quality, service and speed."[11] As such, it is most appropriate for corporations facing drastically changed environmental realities. Often these companies are unable to adapt to these changes because of functional (specialization) rigidities. In other words, reengineering is best suited for businesses in the Institutional phase that have reached the limits of their ability to adapt their functional structure.

Reengineering, in effect, wipes the slate clean and starts over. An organization may, for instance, decide to abolish functional units and create something substantially different. This is a marked departure from the matrix approach, which merely adjusts the existing structure to accommodate environmental changes. Reengineering requires starting from a desired future state and working backward, completely redesigning the entire system.

Such radical change does not come without pain. If a matrix creates problems for those people who cannot easily accommodate complexity, imagine how much more acute is the distress of a total reengineering. And often a reengineering project is but one step in an ongoing process; reengineering can become a way of life.

Are corporations and managers destined to lurch from one reengineering to another? Can we avoid these painful episodes, even though they can generate impressive results?

There is another way. Corporations grounded in the Diversity Management process have the tools to avoid—or at least minimize—the need for restructuring. Managers guided by the process accept ambiguity, uncertainty, unpredictability, and change as givens. Because they expect that change will occur, they are more likely to keep in touch with their external environment. Because they have learned to be flexible, they are not overwhelmed by external change. They operate in a continuously adaptive mode that allows them to accommodate environmental shifts. As a result, they seldom experience the trauma of a major reengineering.

Action Options With the Diversity Management Process

A company that recognizes the need to modify how its various functions interact with one another has many solutions from which to choose. I have described three: using a separate entity (a person or a department) to coordinate between functions; applying a matrix structure; and a full reengineering.

Because each has linkages to the Diversity Management process, the process can serve as an enabler for these solutions. But it offers more as well. Holding the process up to the problem creates the potential for finding other ways to address cross-functional coordination.

Diversity Mixtures and Action Options

A critical first step in the Diversity Management process is to define the existing mixtures and to assess any diversity tension that is present. Clearly the functions themselves constitute a diversity mixture. Once a manager acknowledges the reality of the mixture, she must quickly move to assess the degree of interdependence, and the nature and quantity of diversity tension. If tension is present and is disruptive, the answer may be to integrate the functions in some way.

The manager will need to consider these questions:

- What is the corporation's mission and vision?
- What is our strategy for realizing this mission and vision?
- Given mission, vision, and strategy, what are the key factors that will determine success?
- In light of mission, vision, strategy, and key success factors, what (if any) are the crucial interdependencies between functions?
- What degree of integration is needed, and what mechanisms should be used to bring it about?
- What should be the plan of implementation?

The conclusions from this analysis will determine the manager's response to diversity mixtures. If she concludes that some action is necessary to achieve integration between functions, the Diversity Paradigm can help her think through her options:

Exclude (avoid):	This is the extreme case where a manager does not recognize the mixture. She operates as if on an island; her only world is that of the function. This works only under conditions of a stable environment and an extremely low level of functional interdependence.
Include:	The manager realizes that she is part of a mixture of functions that are different and similar in many ways. From this realization, she must now determine how much specialization is needed and how much collaboration, and identify the organizational arrangements required to achieve them.
Deny:	The manager acknowledges mixtures but discounts the differences

among the functions. His rationale may be, "We all work for the same company. If we keep this in mind, we should be able to work together." This view minimizes functional complexity and allows the manager to act as if there are no significant differences. Whether this will work depends on how dynamic the environment is and how interdependent the functions are. This option cannot be sustained with dynamic environments and interdependent functions.

Isolate: Functional managers realize they are part of a mixture, but one characterized by low interdependence and a relatively stable external environment. Here, the minimal interaction required is achieved through a common boss, procedures, and/or policies. All of the integration is external to the individual units, so their internal dynamics are not disturbed.

Suppress: The manager acknowledges the mixture and the differences among the functions but slips his awareness from this consciousness. As a consequence, he, like the denying manager, can operate as if there were minimal differences among the functions. This is an unstable posture in the midst of a dynamic external environment and/or moderate to high functional interdependence.

Assimilate:	Efforts are made to assimilate all functions into the mold of whatever function is dominant. "No doubt about it, we are a marketing company. Marketing calls the shots." Conflicts are minimized, but so is integration. A real danger is that the required specialization might be compromised.
Tolerate:	Functional managers acknowledge the mixture and the differences among the functions and reluctantly seek to bring about the necessary integration, preferably without disturbing the internal workings of each unit. Relationships among the functions are tentative. "If we *really* must interact, OK—but I would prefer not to."
Build relationships:	As external environments become more dynamic and the need for interdependence increases, managers elect to learn more about each other's functions and the organizational options for bringing about appropriate relationships. This response sets the stage for the relatively intense integration that characterizes mutual adaptation.
Foster mutual adaptation:	This option is appropriate where functional interdependence is high. Managers seek integration of mindsets as well as actions and pursue it through a wide variety of mechanisms: policies/procedures, individuals, structural arrangements,

culture, mission, and vision. The
integration effort is comprehensive.

A number of other diversity mixtures are subordinate to
the mixture of functions. They are subordinate because how
the manager approaches them is determined by how he addressed the functional mixture. Examples of such mixtures
are goals, interpersonal orientations, time orientation, and
degree of formality. The dynamics of addressing these mixtures should parallel those related to the functional mixture.

Another critical mixture in many cases is that of function
and corporate perspectives. In many settings, managers will
have to make appropriate use of both perspectives but not
necessarily simultaneously. However, the more dynamic the
external environment, the greater the functional interdependence; and the greater the functional specialization, the
greater the likelihood that managers will have to adopt both
perspectives simultaneously and will have to do so in an environment that encourages significant gaps between the two.
Here again, working with this mixture of two sometimes contradictory perspectives can be facilitated by the Diversity Paradigm:

Exclude (avoid):	Sees no need to be concerned about both perspectives. This option works only where external environments are stable and functional interdependence is low.
Include:	Acknowledges the need to use both perspectives and essentially creates the mixture. The next step is to determine how and when to use each.
Deny:	Recognizes the need to use both mixtures, but minimizes the differences between the two. "What's good for the company is good for the function; what's good for the

Isolate:

Suppress:

Assimilate:

Tolerate:

function is good for the company." When specialization and interdependence are high and the external environment is changing, this posture can be dysfunctional.

Alternates between each perspective. With relatively stable external environments, low interdependence, and low specialization, this sequential isolation offers minimum risk. However, with high functional specialization and dynamic environments, the gap between corporate and functional perspectives can become significant and can necessitate the wearing of both hats simultaneously.

Suppresses the differences between the two perspectives from her consciousness. This allows her to act as if it makes no difference which one she uses. Minimal functional specialization, interdependence, and stable environments allow this option to be viable.

Assimilates the corporate perspective into that of the functional, or the functional perspective into that of the corporate. Either way, assimilation eliminates the differences and allows this manager to act as if the two perspectives are equivalent. If functional specialization and interdependence are high and the external environment is dynamic, assimilation is dysfunctional.

Recognizes and accepts the legiti-

	macy of both perspectives but does so reluctantly. Functional managers understand the need to incorporate the corporate perspective, and corporate managers appreciate the need to have functional perspectives, but they embrace the others' view tentatively and minimally. This option becomes inappropriate as environments become more dynamic and interdependence becomes greater.
Build relationships:	Both corporate and functional managers elect to explore in depth each other's perspectives, with a particular eye to differences and similarities and their implication for organizational arrangements. The analysis may make managers more aware of the need to use each perspective sequentially, or to develop the ability to draw from both simultaneously. If the latter is the conclusion, the stage is set for mutual adaptation.
Foster mutual adaptation:	An integrated framework is developed that reflects both perspectives. This likely will be a stretch for individuals accustomed to wearing one hat at a time. This option makes most sense under conditions of high functional specialization and interdependence, as well as a dynamic external environment.

Coming to grips with this diversity mixture can facilitate both corporate-function and function-function relationships.

If they learn to appreciate the corporate perspective, functional managers are more likely to understand the importance of quality relationships among the functions.

What follows is a look at one corporation's reengineering efforts in the context of functional dynamics and the Diversity Management process.

The Hallmark Story*

In 1990, Hallmark Cards began a major reengineering process. This process, christened the "Journey of Continuous Improvement," has been highly successful. Notable for our purposes is the way in which certain elements of the Hallmark process mirror elements of the Diversity Management process and can be defined in this context.

Background

The Hallmark of today is a far cry from the postcard business started in 1910 by eighteen-year-old Joyce C. Hall in a room at the Kansas City, Missouri, YMCA. With 1994 sales in excess of $3 billion, privately held Hallmark Cards, Inc., owns a commanding lead over its nearest competitors in the "personal expressions" business. Such success, however, has not been achieved and maintained through complacency.

In 1985, Hallmark executives faced a complex situation. With more than 40 percent of the U.S. greeting card market, their company was clearly doing well. The organization enjoyed several significant strengths. It was both strong and profitable. It had a long-standing commitment to maintaining employment, and its corporate culture had always placed a high value on excellence.

*This case is developed from material provided by Hallmark Cards, Inc., and interviews with company representatives. Also, information was gleaned from Hammer and Champy's study of Hallmark that is included in their *Reengineering the Corporation*.

Yet, Hallmark was experiencing dramatic shifts in the business environment. Customer profiles were changing, the market was fragmenting, and retail outlets were increasing in numbers and types.

Of particular concern was the diversity and complexity of the Hallmark consumer. "We used to know our customers in our bones," says Irvine O. Hockaday, Jr., Hallmark's president and chief executive officer. "She was a housewife who shopped in a suburban mall, where Hallmark had many of its card shops. But by 1985, a 'typical' card buyer no longer existed. 'She' might just as easily be a divorced 'he' shopping in a discount store for a card to send his step-brother's wife."

Robert L. Stark, former president of Hallmark's Personal Communications Group, as it was then called, recalls, "The number of stock-keeping units was expanding far faster than our sales rate, and our average printing run sizes were falling. These changes were affecting the economies of our business."[12]

Company executives began a lengthy period of self-assessment. What emerged from the assessment was a strategic plan that Stark conceptualizes as "much like peeling an onion. The idea was to start on the outside and work our way in—from marketing strategy to organizational structure to operating practices."

In Diversity Management's terms, environmental circumstances that differed greatly from the status quo to which Hallmark's executives had become accustomed resulted in diversity tension. This tension in turn prompted self-analysis, which in turn resulted in the launching of a strategic response—in this case, reengineering. (Reengineering, while addressing the dramatically increased complexity the company was experiencing, created additional complexity of its own.)

Strategy

Hallmark executives faced a multifaceted strategic task. They not only had to develop and implement a new marketing strategy; they had to create a plan for mobilizing 21,000 employees to re-create the organization as well.

They determined early on that ongoing communication and education would be key. These efforts were to center around both the stability of the company's core values and beliefs and the necessity for and reasons why major aspects of the company must change.

Hallmark chairman Donald J. Hall, CEO Hockaday, and other senior executives addressed the task over several months through individual and group meetings, videos, and corporate publications.[13] In the 1989 Winter issue of *Crown*, the company's quarterly magazine, Hall wrote:

> For all of its nearly eighty years, Hallmark has operated under a set of beliefs and values that have guided our business practices. But we haven't always talked about them that much. They were defined more by actions and example than by words. Today, however, there are compelling reasons to talk about them. . . . (1) In the ongoing journey of change, we must look to our beliefs and values to guide us and to anchor us. . . . (2) Our values are the only things that ultimately will protect us from making mistakes that would undermine our reputation, our integrity and, therefore, our success.

He then articulated a list of beliefs and values that were widely disseminated throughout the organization.

In Diversity Management terms, the focus on communication was an effort to develop the individual mindsets that would support reengineering by helping employees recognize the reality of environmental change and reconcile this reality with the comfort of the status quo. This step was critical. Without it, longtime Hallmarkers would have had great difficulty reconciling their status quo view of reality with that being described by company officials.

Communication efforts also detailed the parameters of

THIS IS HALLMARK

We believe:

That our products and services must enrich people's lives and enhance their relationships;

That creativity and quality—in our concepts, products and services—are essential to our success;

That the people of Hallmark are our company's most valuable resource;

That distinguished financial performance is a must, not as an end in itself, but as a means to accomplish our broader mission;

That our private ownership must be preserved.

The values that guide us are:

Excellence in all we do,

Ethical and moral conduct at all times and in all our relationships,

Innovation in all areas of our business as a means of attaining and sustaining leadership,

Corporate social responsibility to Kansas City and to each community in which we operate.

These beliefs and values guide our business strategies, our corporate behavior, and our relationships with suppliers, customers, communities, and each other.

---

the corporate perspective (the hat) that managers would be expected to have in addition to those of their units. To put this in terms we used in Chapter 5, communications also served to affirm the elements of the psychological contract that would not change and those that would.

Isolation also was a key aspect of Hallmark's initial change strategy. Executives developed and piloted selected process redesign plans.

When the pilots proved successful, the reengineering process continued. The focus shifted to diffusing process redesign throughout the corporation. That is, the focus turned to *assimilating* the nonpilot sites around process redesign.

To do this, managing functional relationships became critical. As noted earlier in this chapter, when task environments become diverse, they often create interdependencies among functions that previously had been relatively independent. This happened at Hallmark.

"It was obvious early on that this had to be a company-wide effort because it required cross-divisional teamwork of a magnitude we had never experienced before," Stark recalls. "We had been improving as a functionally oriented company for some time. But if we were going to make real breakthroughs and change the fundamental way we did business, the changes would have to occur across all these functions. It required a level of connection and cooperation that had not been required in the past."[14]

Hallmark's executives agreed that the level of change desired could best be achieved through a top-down approach. They recognized support for the effort was not likely to reach a critical mass on its own or to grow from the bottom up.[15]

The first step in expanding reengineering was to appoint a transition team representing twelve major functions. Team members were charged with identifying opportunities for major change in the way that Hallmark operated.

In the context of the Diversity Management process, implementation of reengineering at Hallmark required penetration of the functional silo walls. Interdependencies dictated a *mutual adaptation* approach to integration. This was necessary because the process design adjustments to environmental shifts could not take place without massive cross-functional effort. Cross-functional teams became the major integrative vehicle for securing cross-functional collaboration. The use of these teams meant that Hallmark's managers would encounter more diversity and complexity than had been the case in the past.

Integrative devices were used to facilitate cross-functional process redesign. The first, designed to enhance the effectiveness of team process, was team building or, in Diversity Management terms, relationship building. The second was to use spatial arrangements to foster the effectiveness of cross-divisional and cross-functional teams.

Wayne Herran, Hallmark vice president for operations, described some of the major changes that took place in the graphic arts divisions when he was its head.

The pilot program had shown the biggest time eater to be "queue" time. So Herran set out to eliminate as much of this wasted time as possible. "The solution was to break apart the silos of specialties," he explained. "We formed new teams by picking one or two members from each of the six specialties. We made sure that every team had at least one member who could perform all the functions necessary to produce the film from which the card is printed. Now, if there's a question, people just ask the person sitting next to them."

Herran did, in fact, literally remove the walls in the graphic arts department and replace them with chest-high cubicles. That way, he reasoned, workers could ask questions of each other without leaving their seats.

The results speak for themselves: The average time required for a card to go through the department is down from forty days to three days. The cycle for wrapping paper has been cut from eighty to eight days.

Finally, substantial training programs were introduced to foster continued diffusions of process redesign. Program objectives have been to help employees approach their work from the process redesign perspective and to provide specific skills in effective team building, decision making, and problem solving. Additional training focuses on group dynamics—attacking problems in a group, brainstorming techniques, and understanding the differences in people's perceptions. Managerial leadership courses have focused on teaching managers new ways of doing their jobs. The overall goal is to achieve more effective working relationships.

Hallmark has even begun to apply the teamwork concept to its outside suppliers. The merchandising division created a key-supplier program designed to reduce the number of suppliers used and to create strong partnerships with those of highest quality. These alliances with fewer suppliers enable Hallmark to create higher-quality products and contain costs.

Issues Related to Business Process Reengineering

Hallmark's process redesign has dramatically altered the lives of its employees, and senior managers have been careful to address all dimensions of its impact. They recognized from the outset that they were asking people to alter their perspectives on numerous aspects of their work lives.

Key to this altering of employee perspectives was the redefining of three critical concepts:

1. Excellence, a core value at Hallmark, traditionally was defined as a *goal* to be achieved. The Continuous Improvement concept redefines excellence as a *process.*
2. The definition of *customer* has been expanded to include everyone inside and outside the company. This redefinition makes each stage in the business process responsible for providing the best possible services and products to the next stage.
3. Managers are asked to give up their role as "supervisors" in exchange for that of "facilitators."

An additional impact on Hallmark's managers is the reduced need for traditional mid-level management. Wayne Herran's experience with the graphic arts department is typical. "A few years ago, there were 130 middle managers for this 1,000-person division," he explains. "Now we have only 85. However, no one was laid off as a result of lack of work. Most have been reassigned, preferably in similar jobs or similar-paying jobs."

Hallmark executives are adamant that faster production, not personnel reduction, is a driving force behind the redesign effort. Herran notes that the graphic arts department now handles twice the card designs it did in 1985 with the same number of people.

Management's message to all employees has been, "Continuous Improvement doesn't mean working harder and faster. It means thinking about why we do things the way we do—and how we can do them better." Hallmark managers admit that employee acceptance has been a major challenge. "As business processes are accelerated," Stark said, "our people need to understand that we aren't asking them to take the quality out of the product. If it really adds value to the consumer, then we want to put more of it in. But that isn't always the same as adding cost."

Impact of Teams

Team members at Hallmark agree that the team structure enables them to make breakthrough accomplishments. The teams have brought together numerous individuals from diverse backgrounds and allowed them to think through each step of their projects without regard to what can't be done. Team members have learned about steps that come before and after their part in the development process. They have applied technology and other new concepts in their work. And, they report, they have broadened their skills and understanding.

Overall, enthusiasm for working in teams is high. Some people report feeling more passionate about their work because they understand all the steps in the process, and everyone owns the outcome. Others point out that the accuracy and quality of work goes up when fewer hands handle a job. Team members are much more knowledgeable than they were when each individual was expected to do his/her part of the job and then pass it on.

In Sum

The Hallmark case offers a classic example of how shifting environmental realities can modify interdependencies and relationships among functions. We have used the Diversity Management process as a lens for examining Hallmark's experiences with reengineering and have demonstrated that it is helpful in exploring functional relationship issues. Perhaps more important is the implication that the process can be used to enable managers to cope effectively with functional specialization and integration.

8

The True Meaning
of Globalism: Diversity
# of Nations
Case Study: EDS

Globalism is unadulterated complexity. As corporations and their managers seek to go global, questions abound. How do customs differ in unfamiliar lands? How can we prepare employees for global service? What are the most effective marketing strategies in the various geographic locations? How will we manage workforce diversity of a much greater magnitude than we experience with domestic employees alone? How will we simultaneously implement multiple strategies reflecting global complexity and global competitive realities? Most important, how will we meld a multinational operation into a unified, globally focused, competitive business enterprise? The skill with which a company addresses these questions will determine how well it realizes its global potential.

Global complexity manifests itself through two types of diversity mixtures: those shared with other major transformation efforts and those unique to globalism. Learning, change, and workforce diversity mixtures, for example, are critical to globalism. But they're common to other transformation efforts as well. What is different for most domestic companies going global is the magnitude of the transformation necessary with respect to mindsets, organization culture, and systems (resource allocation, strategic planning, selection, measurement, rewards, and development).

Global Diversity Mixtures

Going global can be conceptualized as a Diversity Management process. It involves a varied, complicated series of diversity mixtures and related diversity tensions. Some of the mixtures are described here.

Mixture of Opportunities

Companies anticipating going abroad must deal initially with the diversity mixture of domestic possibilities and global possibilities. This mixture always exists for domestic corporations but is of little significance as long as domestic possibilities offer the most potential. Diversity tension becomes substantial when domestic opportunities become relatively scarce. This tension forces you to place importance on the mixture and to determine an appropriate approach. One way to do that is to work through the eight action options of the Diversity Paradigm:

Include:	Managers pursue both domestic and global possibilities. Typically, they begin by "going international" in a limited way, setting up operations in one or two foreign countries.
Exclude:	"We don't need to do anything global." This option is most likely to be exercised when decision makers see domestic potential remaining markedly greater, believe that their hands are full with realizing domestic potential, feel intimidated

by their lack of knowledge about global markets, or believe that they lack sufficient resources to pursue seriously both sets of opportunities.

Deny: Managers deny any differences between domestic and global opportunities, assuming that domestic and global markets are much more alike than different. So, if resources permit, they see no reason not to pursue global possibilities.

Isolate: Managers decide to proceed, but in an isolated fashion, by setting up an international division headquartered in the domestic corporate office. This allows them to test global possibilities with minimum disruption of domestic operations.

Assimilate: "Let's proceed." Managers who choose this option believe that while there are significant differences in the opportunities, the global ones can be assimilated so that they can operate as they do domestically. This option can coexist well with denial.

Suppress: "Let's proceed." These managers think that while there are differences, participants in the international arena will suppress them, so they will be able to do business as they do in the United States. Or they may note differences and then, unable to deal with the related complexity, opt to suppress.

Tolerate: "Let's do it, if we really must." Here, managers decide on the grounds of realism, practicality, and economic necessity to proceed, but they never embrace the decision emotionally. Under these conditions, international operations will remain step-children.

Build relationships: "Let's do it, but slowly and carefully. Let's learn as much as we can about global sites, so that our operations will be grounded in a solid understanding of the locations where we will do business." Here, understanding and sensitivity are viewed as critical to global success. This option might be used with isolation and toleration.

Foster mutual adaptation: Managers decide to proceed with a clear awareness that major changes in ways of doing business will be required. They see the need for a unified operation that takes advantage of domestic and global opportunities simultaneously. They understand that this unified operation might differ significantly from their current domestic organization.

Historically, U.S. companies going global have usually relied on isolation, denial, assimilation, and suppression.[1] This resulted in complaints that Americans did not understand the lands where they were doing business and were not positioned to be particularly effective. These complaints produced an emphasis on responsiveness and sensitivity to local conditions. Over the years, several articles and books have surfaced to guide executives in managing across cultures.[2] For a while, in fact, reverse assimilation was seen as most appropriate—when in Rome, do as the Romans do.

Currently, a company's first global operation is more likely to reflect a combination of isolation, toleration, and relationship building. Separate international divisions are set up with the idea that *local responsiveness,* achieved through toleration and building relationships, will be the key to strategic, competitive advantage.

Mixture of Nations

A related, but different, diversity mixture is that of multiple nations. As corporations set up units around the world or plan global expansion, they create a mixture of nations where they are doing business, nations with differences and similarities in history, politics, culture, market characteristics, and potential. Companies must decide how to relate to various units in multiple nations or regions.

A triggering diversity tension may come when managers encounter negative consequences as a result of not acknowledging differences. International participants may, for example, complain about attempts to make "one size fit all"—using standard domestic procedures in all foreign operations.

Diversity tension can also emerge when an offshore site is successful. Site managers begin to assert that the company could make "real money" if it became serious about international operations. "Becoming serious" often translates into acting on the knowledge that core adaptations may be needed—a clear source of tension.

Whatever the motivation, the question remains, how should we respond to this mixture? Again, the Diversity Paradigm provides guidance:

Exclude (avoid):   Any exclusion at this juncture is likely to be on economic grounds. Countries that lack evidence of appropriate revenue and profit potential are excluded.

Isolate: This option can be exercised for individual nations and for groups of nations that share commonalities. When exercised for an individual nation, the units in each nation are grouped and treated as one autonomous entity. When exercised for groups of nations, units within countries that share political, cultural, historical, and market similarities are treated as single entities—separate from both the home and other group entities.

Deny: Here, managers see few significant national differences, so they see little need to grant national units autonomy or to group them by geographic regions. Local responsiveness is not a strategic consideration.

Assimilate: Differences are recognized but perceived as unimportant. Managers assume that the locals will assimilate to the taste reflected in the company's products, or to some normative concept of a customer profile. They see little need to grant autonomy.

Suppress: Managers assume that international units and their participants will be open to suppressing differences. Or they may recognize differences but suppress this awareness, and therefore see little need to differentiate among nations. This can work if the locals are not assertive about their differences.

Tolerate: This option represents a cautious
                           acknowledgement and accommo-
                           dation of differences. "If we really
                           must, we'll take the differences into
                           account through national auton-
                           omy or regional groupings." Reluc-
                           tantly, an awareness evolves that
                           differences and similarities must be
                           considered as organizing options
                           are selected. However, managers
                           hope to do this without disturbing
                           the domestic status quo.

Build relationships: "Let's at least get to know each
                           other better in case there are oppor-
                           tunities for synergy." Seeking
                           greater understanding can reaffirm
                           the wisdom of isolation, or it can
                           call for major restructuring toward
                           a unified, global enterprise. The
                           thinking here is the more we know
                           each other, the more things will be
                           OK. "OK" can mean moving
                           toward mutual adaptation or main-
                           taining the status quo.

Foster mutual adaptation: "Let's meld all the national enter-
                           prises into a focused, unified global
                           effort." Here, the new organization
                           would reflect differences and simi-
                           larities, but as a part of a global
                           whole, and not in the context of
                           loosely connected autonomous eco-
                           nomic units. This is the only option
                           requiring a truly global approach.
                           It presumes a willingness on the
                           part of the corporation and local
                           participants to be open to adapta-

tion and to deal with diversity and complexity.

Mixture of Strategies

Once differences are accepted as significant, a popular action option has been local responsiveness through isolation. Local enterprises within the various countries are granted considerable autonomy. Regional groupings whose circumstances differ from those of other regions are granted decision-making latitude as well. Implicit in these arrangements is an assumption that local responsiveness is strategic to competitive advantage. These practices will continue until other strategic factors compromise the importance of this option.

If managers don't accept differences as significant, they place little priority on organizing around geographic locations. They organize, instead, around products or functions. Implicitly, they assume that local responsiveness is not a strategic factor.

It is more likely, however, that, rather than adopt an "either/or" approach to gaining competitive advantage, managers will look at "both/and"—local responsiveness *and* product innovation or functional competence.[3] Managers who adopt a "both/and" perspective immediately encounter another diversity mixture: at least three strategies with differences and similarities—local responsiveness, product innovation, and functional competence.

The triggering diversity tension here is a declining competitive posture. A corporation using one of the three strategies might find itself satisfactorily competitive for a time. As long as the strategy proves effective, the strategic diversity mixture is irrelevant. But when signs indicate a weakening vitality of the given strategy, the mixture of strategies becomes most critical and complexity increases. The Diversity Management process can illuminate the options that managers have at this point:

Include/exclude: The presence of diversity tension makes exclusion a bad choice. Failure to draw on all three options can produce dire results.

Deny: Managers use all three strategies without recognizing differences among them. Massive denial of the differences among them is required and implementation is difficult or impossible.

Isolate: Managers frequently employ "sequential isolation," rotating from one strategy to another. The challenge is to know when and how to do so. This has been a popular practice. But consensus is growing that each option has its advantages and limitations, and that none by itself gives sustainable competitive advantage. What is optimal is the *simultaneous* use of all three strategies.[4]

Suppress: Managers recognize and understand the differences among the strategies but suppress this awareness. Suppression is as unlikely to work as denial and for the same reasons.

Assimilate: Managers select from each strategy the elements that are compatible with the other two, or at least with the dominant strategy. This minimizes complexity and facilitates implementation. But the integrity of each is compromised, and the result is less than optimal. The assim-

	ilated blend is much less than the sum of the parts.
Tolerate:	Managers organize primarily around one strategic option, but supplement it with components from one or both of the remaining two. This is a selective, cautious embracing of all three strategies.
Build relationships:	Managers strive to understand each strategy thoroughly in hopes of determining what linkages disturb the status quo least, on the assumption that it is these that work best. They may determine that linkages are possible and can be effective without compromising any of the strategies, or that linkages are not likely and mutual adaptation is necessary.
Foster mutual adaptation:	Managers work to create arrangements (structural and otherwise) that allow the simultaneous use of all three strategic options, in order to gain maximum benefit.

Isolation, toleration and mutual adaptation have been the most popular options for strategic diversity. Most companies appear to rely heavily on the toleration option. Academic prescriptions call increasingly for a mutual adaptation approach. Managers have acknowledged the need to do this for some time. The challenge has been implementation.

When organizations aspire to mutual adaptation, they frequently stumble over the complexity of the transformation process. Another common problem is reliance on structural changes—in particular the matrix model—as their *only* lever for implementation.[5] The need to use more than one lever simultaneously has become increasingly clear. Avoiding complexity is not an option.

People Diversity Mixture

Companies that go global must expect enormous work force diversity. Global additions incorporate national and regional differences in language, culture, values, religion, priorities and time orientation. The more global coordination and communication become strategically critical, the more pronounced tension related to this diversity becomes. This is particularly evident when individuals from different functions and regions must work together as teams. The possible action options are:

Include: The manager acknowledges the workforce as a mixture of employees from all global locations. By definition, inclusion is the only option for corporations aspiring to be global.

Exclude: By definition, managers aspiring to globalization are limited in their use of this option. A form of exclusion occurs, however, when senior executives send domestic managers to fill key slots around the world.

Deny: Denial can occur in at least two ways. Company executives can act as if they have only a domestic workforce and develop plans and systems in this context of massive denial. Alternately, they may base their actions on the reality of a diverse world workforce but deny that people within this workforce are different. They reason that "people are people wherever you find them."

Isolate: A significant form of isolation occurs when managers confine individuals to their geographic origin. This isolation practice minimizes workforce complexity but limits employees' career options and the corporation's ability to utilize talents.

Suppress: People are encouraged to downplay their differences in the presence of corporate personnel or others who are not from their geographic location. Another possibility is that people are permitted to demonstrate their differences, with the manager acknowledging these differences but then suppressing his awareness of them.

Assimilate: Managers expect individuals to adopt the practices of corporate headquarters. They, for example, may encourage talented individuals to accept a tour of duty in the home office to facilitate their assimilation and prepare them for greater responsibility.

Tolerate: Members of the headquarters group accept but never embrace differences. They may, for example, discuss differences in a condescending, patronizing way but not take them into account when making policy or evolving practices. They listen to but never hear people from other geographic areas. Theirs is a superficial acceptance of workforce complexity.

Build relationships: Often accompanying assimilation

and suppression, this option seeks harmony and minimization of differences among employees from all regions by fostering relationships. People from the dominant geographic location visit other sites to gain understanding. Employees from other areas visit the dominant location for the same purpose. This practice often produces reverse assimilation and suppression, thus reaffirming the notion that "people are people." What often gets confirmed, however, is that people can share similarities while simultaneously demonstrating significant differences. Acknowledgement of this reality sets the stage for mutual adaptation.

Foster mutual adaptation: This option gives rise to the creation of a unified global managerial process that acknowledges and incorporates the reality of a global workforce characterized by differences and similarities. Under this arrangement, hiring decisions reflect the reality that new hires can serve eventually anywhere around the world, regardless of where they were recruited. Similarly, for a manager seeking to fill a position from within, the pool consists of qualified candidates from around the world.

Mixture of Proven Capabilities

As a company's international operations prove their viability, managers must confront a mixture of proven domestic *and* international capabilities. This creates a need to shift from, or at least complement, the local responsiveness strategy.

Managers at the international site typically stress geographical differences and arrangements, while those at the domestic location view product innovation and functional efficiency and effectiveness as key strategic factors. As these managers press to bring international operations under a domestic product and/or functional structure, diversity tensions mount.

Diversity tension increases as the international site experiences greater success. The more critical the revenue and profits from the international arena, the more likely that power struggles will emerge.[6] Domestic divisions, fearful of being upstaged by their international cohorts, mount calls to bring the international enterprise under a domestic product or functional structure.

Popular action options for addressing this challenge include:

Deny:	It's possible to deny differences between the capabilities until the diversity tension becomes so great that this becomes impractical. Turbulent global or domestic environments will accommodate this option for only a limited time.
Isolate:	People at the international site often favor this option. It keeps their turf intact and preserves their power. They emphasize how different it is to do business abroad and how important it is to isolate, maintain, and nourish this expertise.
Suppress:	Recognizing and suppressing the differences between the proven capabilities works for only as long as the environments allow it to be practical.

Assimilate: People at the domestic location are
                                 most likely to favor this option.
                                 Managers who believe that product
                                 innovation is *the* key strategic factor
                                 argue for worldwide structural ar-
                                 rangements; those who see func-
                                 tional competencies as the key call
                                 for worldwide functional struc-
                                 tures. Both of these scenarios allow
                                 for subunit geographic structures,
                                 but these structures lose much of
                                 the clout that they would enjoy
                                 under the isolation option. Assimi-
                                 lation maintains or enhances the
                                 power enjoyed by domestic-loca-
                                 tion personnel.

Tolerate: Managers recognize both capabili-
                                 ties and seek ways to take both into
                                 account without committing to too
                                 much change. The dominant capa-
                                 bility remains dominant, but lip
                                 service is given to exploiting both
                                 capabilities.

Build relationships: Managers are reluctant to make
                                 major structural changes that would
                                 significantly alter the arrangements
                                 of both capabilities. Instead, they
                                 seek to earnestly understand both
                                 and to build linkages. Most of these
                                 linkages—common reporting ar-
                                 rangements, task forces, or integrat-
                                 ing departments, for example—are
                                 external to the entities. If these ar-
                                 rangements don't work, the stage is
                                 set for mutual adaptation.

Foster mutual adaptation: The strengths and weaknesses of
                                 the domestic and international

sides are integrated into a unified, global entity. Cultural roots, values, and systems are unified in the new entity, and all levels have substantial influence. This global entity is neither domestic nor international. It is, instead, a totally different enterprise, focused on global realities.

The Emerging Global Model

The classic global model prescribed a company with centralized management and a vision of a unified, relatively homogeneous market across the world. Foreign subsidiaries were seen as delivery pipelines.[7] Diversity among the markets was deemed irrelevant, because of either denial or assumptions that those in international markets were willing to be assimilated or to suppress their differences.

Increasingly, however, there is talk of a new global corporate model.[8] This model prescribes that companies maintain an integrated, focused global perspective but accept the reality and legitimacy of diversity (complexity) mixtures and build around them. In terms of the Diversity Paradigm, we might say: *The global corporation relies on mutual adaptation to address the diversity mixtures associated with realizing the full potential of doing business on a global scale.* Mutual adaptation is the action option with the maximum capability to deal with complexities.

This new global model differs from the "delivery" model in several ways. The classic model sought to deliver standard domestic products to the rest of the world; the new one seeks to provide the best possible products in the most efficient way to wherever it does business. The new model acknowledges that the best product for one location may not be optimal for another. It acknowledges the need for "fit" between product and location, and posits product flexibility and customization as key to responsiveness to local conditions.

The new model views diversity—that is, complexity—as a legitimate given. The nationalism surfacing in many countries negates the option of denying differences or assuming assimilation or suppression, as the classic model implicitly did.

The classic model featured centralized decision making. The new corporate model prescribes simultaneous centralization and decentralization to ensure implementation of multiple strategies. The classic managerial focus emphasized command and control; the new one relies on empowerment to facilitate local responsiveness.

The new model calls for an organizational vision that incorporates the characteristics of a unified global company. Developing and embedding this vision throughout the organization is critical.

As with any major organizational change, compatible basic assumptions (roots) are essential for effective globalization.[9] Domestic roots (monocountry, monocultural) provide a poor foundation for multicountry, multicultural operations. Yet, replacing domestic roots with global or transnational ones can be traumatic. Selectivity, timing, and education are key to any root-changing process.

In sum, the new global model exploits local responsiveness, product innovations, and functional effectiveness and efficiencies as sources of competitive advantage. The classic model relied singularly on the effective, efficient delivery of goods.

Many American companies operate around the world, but few are genuinely global. To go global is to develop the organizational capability to cope with global diversity mixtures. As Exhibit 8-1 illustrates, there is a distinct difference between doing business internationally and being a global corporation.

Exhibit 8-1. A comparison of the major elements of the old and new global models.

Variable	Old Global Model	New Global Model
Objective	Deliver domestic products worldwide	Deliver best possible products to all locations
Diversity	Illegitimate	Legitimate
Market	Unified, no allowance for diversity	Unified, with allowance for diversity
Products	Standardized domestic	Product flexibility
Managerial focus	Command to control	Empowerment
Systems	Unified, no allowance for diversity	Unified, allowance for diversity
Shared vision	Domestic	Global
Roots	Domestic	Global
Sources of competitive advantage	Effective and efficient delivery of goods	Multiple • Local responsiveness • Product Innovation • Function efficiency and effectiveness

The EDS Story*

EDS, a major corporation and industry leader, provides an example of a company developing specific plans for becoming a global organization. It also is an excellent example of the evolution in thinking that occurs when people begin working with a wider view of what diversity really means.

EDS considers a global entity as one that can send to *any* customer *anywhere* a team of those professionals best qualified to meet the client's needs. The professionals can be re-

*This case study is based on materials provided by EDS and interviews conducted with EDS personnel.

cruited from any location in global EDS. Their qualifications can relate to technical, industry, market, or geographic expertise. A recent effort to secure a European contract illustrates how global teams might come together. EDS people from seven countries and eleven strategic units on both sides of the Atlantic collaborated for more than six months to secure this opportunity.

Global Parameters

EDS's global environment is characterized by rapid change and requirements for flexibility, risk taking, and innovation. Recognizing that complexity, EDS managers have crafted and adopted a corporate vision reflecting these external realities (see page 185).

Global Strategy

EDS is seeking four global strategic outcomes: (1) sustained growth, (2) expanded market share, (3) status as a defining leader of the industry, and (4) status as a *truly* global corporation.

The company sees its commitment to customers as the source of its competitive advantage in pursuing these strategic outcomes. To maintain this focus, the company uses multiple strategies:

- *The use of smaller business modules* that link the activities of employees to the needs of suppliers and customers.
- *Reliance on teams* rather than individuals to maximize the effectiveness of the work, while simultaneously stressing individual excellence.
- *Learning company spirit.* Remaining customer-focused in a fast-paced environment is impossible without a learning capability. Reeducation and mindset shifts will be continuous.
- *Reliance on a total-quality customer focus.* At the heart of

---

The EDS Vision Statement

Statement of Intent. EDS will be the leader in shaping how information is created, distributed, shared, enjoyed and applied for the benefit of enterprises and individuals worldwide.

Manifestations. We will capitalize on the opportunities of globalization, individualization and informationalization to produce value that contributes to our customers' success and well-being. We will use our core competencies, and those of others, to create this value and to create leverage for EDS.

We will expect each other to contribute our best work and our best thinking and to demonstrate leadership behavior.

We will achieve superior relationships with our customers, produce superior financial results for our shareholders, and merit the loyalty of the EDS team members.

Result. Achieving our intent will cause EDS to be sought out by others as a thought leader, strategic partner, and the provider of choice.

---

total quality is customer focus. The principles of total quality are essential to maintaining a customer focus.
- *Implementation of Managing Diversity.* EDS's capability with diversity as a global factor is evolving and will be discussed later. Of importance here is the company's commitment to embracing diversity in a way that accelerates its global aspirations.

No one implementation thrust could by itself provide the level of achievement that EDS is committed to; all must be used simultaneously. Readers of this book will recognize that

EDS is using a diverse mixture of implementation levers to leverage the globalization process.

Diversity at EDS

As part of its global framework, EDS is evolving a specific diversity process. That process is not yet complete, as the company freely admits. EDS leaders also willingly acknowledge that they experienced some false starts.

EDS began its diversity efforts by addressing workforce diversity in the United States. The initial programs had an "understanding differences" focus, designed to help employees come to grips with natural tendencies to stereotype in terms of race and gender. Then these programs were exported to EDS operations abroad in essentially the same format except that nationality, not race and gender, became the point of analysis.

These programs enjoyed only limited success. Europeans thought it was an American program about an American problem with little relevance to them. The domestic model produced little indication that participants garnered a better understanding of diversity or changed their behaviors as a result of increased awareness. Sponsors pulled the program after eighteen months and returned to the drawing board.

As they wrestled with these specific concerns about implementation, the EDS team found that they actually were coming to grips with more-fundamental questions about diversity. The more closely they looked, the more they saw. Gradually it became clear that what they had been calling diversity was an implicit part of those elements that EDS had already identified as critical for global success. As a result, senior management concluded that diversity was not solely a workforce issue but part and parcel of EDS's global strategy.

The Search for Synergy

At this point EDS leaders instituted a deliberate search for synergy between diversity and the company's global strategy. They began with five objectives:

1. Determine where EDS stands compared to other global corporations and in the context of leading-edge thinking.
2. Establish a framework for and definition of diversity at EDS.
3. Build a compelling case for the importance of diversity.
4. Recommend a plan of action.
5. Determine how to measure progress.

Armed with those incisive objectives, EDS started its search for synergy:

BENCHMARKING: DETERMINING WHERE EDS STOOD. EDS researchers first conducted an internal and an external benchmarking study. From internal sources (EDS executives, diversity champions, and employees), researchers learned that respondents perceived EDS as having no shared vision regarding the meaning of diversity, why it is important, or how to go forward in this arena. But many saw CEO Les Alberthal as genuinely committed to the topic. They also saw current diversity efforts as too focused on race and gender. The consensus seemed to be, "We're not impressed."

External inquiries (comparing notes with several corporations and talking with consultants and academicians) revealed that a few companies were beginning to move beyond race and gender, but none had mastered the global scope challenge. Some corporations, however, had efforts under way to change mindsets at the leadership level.

EXPANDING THE CONCEPT OF DIVERSITY. As they moved to the second objective (defining diversity), the EDS team looked for a way to incorporate their new understanding that diversity is a strategic force contributing to globalism. To verbalize this shift in thinking, they embraced the term *global diversity,* because it implied a diverse set of multiple dimensions. They defined *global diversity* as creating an environment in which:

1. The cultural subconscious of the organization sees strengths in differences.
2. The best ideas and practices from anyone or anywhere are capitalized.
3. Diverse, high-performance teams deliver maximum value to EDS customers and shareholders through creative innovative approaches.
4. Each person has the opportunity to grow and to contribute to his or her fullest potential.

These environmental conditions were viewed as essential for EDS's global success.

The reader should note a critical point here. Diversity has shifted from being an "understanding differences" vehicle for minimizing race and gender tension to a strategic force contributing to globalization.

EDS's exploration leaders cited many reasons for embracing global diversity: more diverse employees, the need for greater efficiency and effectiveness, the critical strategic role of innovation, the ability to transfer know-how, the need to effectively access and/or expand global markets, and the necessity of attracting, developing, and retaining the best people worldwide.

They saw global diversity as important for individuals as well. They believed it was the key to the effective leadership of diverse people in a global workplace, to establishing and maintaining quality relationships, to creating conditions that foster self-realization, and to developing a climate where people can be genuine and valued for who they are.

Global diversity, in sum, would allow EDS to "serve the best customers in the world." Global diversity would be a lever for gaining competitive advantage.

Diversity and Empowered Heterogeneous Teams

One result of EDS's exploration and documentation of environmental complexity is that heterogeneous, empowered teams will augment the individual as a source of competitive advantage. EDS now believes that its ability to deliver quality service depends on its ability to assign the best possible people to a project *anywhere in the world.* Initially, EDS consciously sought to create heterogeneous teams; however, with the company's global business and workforce, diverse teams now evolve naturally. Members of these teams can come from any nation. Obviously, this means they will have many differences. Yet they will be required to form high-performing units that respond quickly to the customers' needs.

EDS people believe that the effectiveness of the heterogeneous teams will be determined by three factors: (1) the degree to which team members can relate to and communicate with each other, (2) the degree of global awareness possessed by a team collectively and individually, and (3) the degree to which EDS's corporate culture is empowering and enabling.

When a team is made up of people from different backgrounds, differences in communication styles will no doubt arise. EDS has focused on certain traits as fundamental to their diversity efforts: humility, trust, self-esteem, curiosity, and empathy. In turn, quality communications must occur in the context of global awareness, of understanding what is taboo or acceptable in given geographic locations. This awareness fosters the capability to be responsive to success requirements across nations.

Finally, to facilitate global awareness and excellence in communication, the corporation's culture must be taken into account. And this consideration will be critical. The decision to elevate the team to the status comparable to the individual represented a significant shift for EDS, where rugged individualism and the image of eagles—which do not flock—have long been rallying points.

EDS, like many corporations, is looking at evolving its corporate culture from a family or patriarchal paradigm to a teamwork-based paradigm. Typically, the family culture includes the following notions:

1. You gain acceptance by being just like me. Assimilation is encouraged and is critical. Differences are seen not as strengths but as problems.
2. You are entitled to the benefits of the organization by virtue of your membership. Simply being an employee means you are due certain benefits.
3. Relationships are hierarchical. You look to your boss for direction and exercise care in acting without his/her approval.
4. The organization takes care of loyal employees. This you can count on.

To promote a more "team-oriented" culture, companies looking to the future are exploring new ideas:

1. You gain acceptance by demonstrating performance or value. Ongoing performance, rather than degree of assimilation, determines the extent of acceptance.
2. Team membership entitles you not to benefits but to an opportunity to earn benefits.
3. Organizational relationships are analogous to those between two adults. Any two team members are peers who relate to each other as adults. Both are empowered to support each other and to contribute to their full potential.
4. Each team member is interdependent with the others and also mutually responsible for the organization's success.

Exhibit 8-2 is a table focusing on the differences between the family and team cultures.

How Much Progress?

In the language of the Diversity Paradigm, we can say that EDS executives are moving to mutual adaptation on a large scale to ensure that their company will be effective as a global

Exhibit 8-2. Family vs. team culture.

Variable	Family Culture	Team Culture
Focus	Individual	Team
Source of acceptance	Emulate boss/ assimilate	Demonstrate performance
Significance of team membership	Provides entitlement to benefits	Provides opportunity to earn benefits
Relationships	Hierarchical	Empowered peers
Basis of rewards	Loyalty	Performance

competitor. They have modified their vision, mission, strategy, and structure to reflect global realities and are now examining the implications of the new globalism for other organizational parameters and practices as well.

Further, EDS has modified its view of diversity to encompass its strategic significance in the globalization process. Given our discussion in the first part of this chapter, we can envision that as EDS progresses with globalization, its leaders will continue to expand their concept of diversity. Also, we can expect that this broadening will move them toward Diversity Management as articulated in this book.

What is valuable here is to note that the company's leaders took the time to secure a conceptual understanding of diversity. As a result, these leaders possess clarity and conviction. But they still must grapple with developing comparable clarity and conviction throughout their organization. They must determine how to best educate their colleagues. Only then can meaningful action planning take place.

All of this means that while it is ahead of most companies, EDS has only just begun the arduous process of defining and addressing global diversity appropriately. The company's leaders are clear on this point. But they also believe that their emerging clarity about the full meaning of diversity gives them a major competitive edge.

9

Managing Toward Seamlessness: Diversity of Strategies
Case Study: Goodyear Tire and Rubber

To respond adequately to today's complex and increasingly competitive environments, managers must adopt complex managerial philosophies and strategies that in turn require complex mindsets and behaviors for implementation. This is an enormous amount of complexity to deal with.

In this chapter we examine the process of coming to grips with multiple layers of complexity through a multifaceted, seamless approach using several managerial strategies simultaneously. Seamlessness means that the collection of various elements are interlinked by an underlying framework and recognized as interdependent in ways that promote synergy. It means no clear-cut dividing line between one strategy and another, but a coherent whole that is greater than the sum of its parts. Seamlessness assists in making complexity manageable.

Complexity involves multiplicity and variations.[1] A complex environment is one characterized by multiple critical elements that differ significantly. A complex philosophy is one that draws from multiple strategies for change levers. Managers searching for the "right" answer often experiment with a variety of approaches at the same time, drawing a combination from the ten strategies highlighted in Exhibit 9-1, plus any others that may gain credibility. This is clearly a dizzying array of options.

Managers who adopt a complex philosophy have an ad-

Exhibit 9-1. Strategic options.

Strategy	Description
• Participatory management	Involves employees in decision making.
• Management by objectives (MBO)	Generates a mutually agreeable performance plan reflecting the manager's expectations and the needs of the individual.
• Total quality management	Advocates a holistic approach to meeting customer needs and expectations efficiently and effectively.
• The learning company	Calls for facilitating the learning of all employees as a vehicle for continuous organizational transformation.
• Reengineering	Provides a framework for bringing about radical change.
• Succession planning	Seeks to ensure continuous development of managerial talent in a timely fashion.
• Diversity Management	Provides a framework for addressing "diversity mixtures" in a manner that maximizes contribution to achievement of business objectives.
• Empowerment	Encourages acceptance and ownership of responsibility for ensuring the organization's continuing viability.
• Culture change	Involves modifying the driving and controling "root" assumptions of an organization.
• Globalism	Involves organizing to exploit opportunities around the world. Manager grounds the organizational system in the organization's global needs, as opposed to its domestic requirements.

ditional task as well. Implementing this philosophy requires an unambivalent buy-in. This, in turn, requires that these managers modify their ways of thinking; they must develop a mindset that reflects the complexity of the appropriate strategic mix. For institutional managers accustomed to proven success formulas, stability, and predictability, this can be most challenging.

Then, having adopted a complex philosophy and mindset, managers must take one additional step forward. They must demonstrate behavior that reflects multiple strategies and adaptability.

Managers seeking to cope with complex environments must "talk" complexity (see, develop, and articulate an appropriately complex managerial philosophy), "think" complexity (adopt mindsets reflecting philosophical complexity) and "walk" complexity (behave in ways compatible with a complex philosophy and mindset). Complex environments require that managers "talk the talk," "think the talk," and "walk the talk." (More about this in Chapter 10.)

It is easy to feel overwhelmed by all this. One way to get a handle on it is to activate the Diversity Management process. If you think of the components of your strategic mix as a diversity mixture, then you can apply the Diversity Paradigm and use it to sort out your options on the various levels.

Defining the Mixtures

The Framework Mixture

A critical macro decision that determines not only how managers will approach the other mixtures but whether they will even be able to consider them is the Institutional/Survival/Business mixture described in Chapter 3. Addressing complexity makes no sense for managers who are operating out of the Institutional or Survival framework. At issue is whether they can move forward to a Business framework.

Diversity Management offers a way for managers to work through this shift. It also offers a way for leaders to coach their managers to the point where the Business framework is firmly and fully adopted.

You may remember that one of the goals of this book is to provide you with opportunities to practice using the Paradigm. I will leave you to apply the eight options of the DM process to the framework mixture.

The Strategic Mixture

In creating a philosophy for addressing environmental complexity, you must select a strategy or combination of strategies to provide the conceptual foundation. The ten strategies in Exhibit 9-1 are a good starting point. You need to consider two overall questions: Which strategies should be used as the philosophical foundation? and, How should they be connected? The Diversity Paradigm can help in the sorting-out process.

Include/exclude: Assuming that the Business framework has been adopted, you will include strategies that relate to environmental realities and exclude (discard or refuse to include) those that do not. Once you have decided what to include, you must identify integrating linkages.

Deny: The manager practicing denial sees the mixture of strategies but does not recognize differences among them. This manager often contends, "If you boil all of these options down to their common denominator, they all are talking about good managing—which we already are doing." The net result here is a perception that it is not necessary to consider utilizing the mixtures—that one approach is essentially as good as another.

Isolate:

The manager decides to keep all ten strategies but to focus on each one separately and sequentially. This manager either proposes a rotating philosophy or selects one for continued focus while subjecting all others to rotation. Rotation is ineffective, on three counts. It does not adequately address complexity, because only one strategy will be fully implemented. In addition, it is likely to generate cynicism about management's seriousness. Finally, the rotating philosophy can give rise to turf wars. With missionary zeal, advocates of one particular strategy take a kill-or-be-killed attitude and fight vigorously for their prescriptions for company viability. Such fights are, of course, divisive.

Suppress:

Advocates of the various strategies are asked to ignore differences and to highlight commonalities with the status quo or with whatever strategy is emerging as dominant. Managers using suppression argue that this will facilitate acceptance and development of a coherent philosophy; often they promise that differences can be resolved later. The danger is that there may never be an opportunity to consider the

Assimilate:

differences. If this happens, the strategies will be compromised severely and the resultant mixture will be inadequate.

Managers who use assimilation take from each strategy whatever pieces fit the status quo or the emerging dominant strategy and then proclaim that they are using all ten strategies. Management by objectives provides a good example of this practice. To listen to managerial rhetoric is to conclude that MBO is widely accepted and practiced. In fact, however, many managers have merely adopted those aspects of MBO that fit their status quo cultures. Assimilation has so watered down MBO that what is practiced varies from one corporation to another depending on the company's culture, and there is widespread confusion as to what MBO really is.

Tolerate:

A manager using toleration will nominally retain all ten strategies but adopt a posture of "include until no longer necessary" toward those that vary from the status quo or emerging dominant strategy. As soon as senior management reduces pressure for the new philosophy, this manager often reverts to the status quo. "See," he says in effect, "I knew we were OK. We now can return to what has made us great all along." Subordinates file

	this experience away as evidence that senior management isn't serious about change or lacks the will to follow through.
Build relationships:	Here managers explore the possibilities of coexistence and ways to achieve synergy, and turf groups minimize their kill-or-be-killed positions. A likely result is a strategy mixture that has the appropriate components but lacks the essential integrating linkages.
Foster mutual adaptation:	This action option goes beyond building relationships. Instead it seeks, by changing culture and supporting systems, to evolve an underlying framework that links the elements together and gives meaning and substance to the philosophy.

In sum, it is becoming increasingly clear that complex, dynamic environments require complex management philosophies using several strategies at the same time. The Diversity Management process makes it clear that the two best ways to achieve this multistrategy approach are to build relationships and foster mutual adaptation.

Using multiple strategies is vastly different from the flavor-of-the-year approach that many managers are coerced into. It means developing new philosophies reflecting environmental complexities, followed by meaningful commitment to their implementation. For institutional managers, in particular, this process can present major difficulties. They are used to focusing on concrete policies and rules; they are not accustomed to wrestling with philosophical issues.

Achieving Seamlessness

Evolving and implementing a multistrategy philosophy appropriate for a complex environment is a daunting undertaking. Indeed, the complexity of conceptualizing, articulating, and acting within the context of such a philosophy suggests why so many transformation efforts fail.

The magnitude of the complexity dictates that a high priority be placed on achieving *seamlessness*. Seamlessness occurs when there is not only an awareness of the interrelationships among a collection of elements but an integrating macro framework that gives cohesiveness to this collective mixture. Such an integrating framework at once minimizes the level of complexity and enhances management's ability to address the complexity that remains.

Most important, articulating meaning in an organization sets the stage for people to connect that meaning with their personal life meanings and thus to become committed.

The Goodyear Story*

Moving Toward Seamlessness

Goodyear Tire and Rubber has helped its most senior managers to collectively develop a multistrategy managerial philosophy and to individually conceptualize, articulate, and act within the framework of this philosophy. The seamlessness that this produces is facilitating the corporation's movement from the institution to the business framework. This case

---

*This case study is drawn from materials provided by Goodyear and also the experiences of the design team in developing the Morehouse course. The following individuals comprised the design team: Steve Drotter of Drotter and Associates, Elizabeth Holmes of the Center for Creative Leadership, R. Roosevelt Thomas, Jr., of The American Institute for Managing Diversity, and from Goodyear: Mark Hartman, Karen Henry, and Jackie Taylor.

study looks at one intervention Goodyear used in pursuit of seamlessness.

Historical Context

Goodyear, founded in Akron, Ohio, in 1898 by Frank Seiberling, began with a product line of bicycle and carriage tires, horseshoe pads, and poker chips. The company prospered and by 1916 had earned the right to the slogan "More people ride on Goodyear tires than on any other kind." By 1926, Goodyear achieved the status of the world's largest rubber company, a distinction it retained until recently.

Goodyear's strategy for achieving these heights has been three-pronged:

1. *The continuous search for new markets and product applications.* Today, Goodyear makes tires for virtually every vehicle except bicycles and offers a wide variety of other product lines.
2. *A willingness to do business around the world.* Approximately half of the company's production facilities are outside of the United States, and sales and distribution operations are located in virtually every nation of the world.
3. *An innovative spirit that has fostered many breakthroughs.*

In 1986, "corporate raider" James Goldsmith attempted to buy the company. Goldsmith argued that the sum of the values of Goodyear's components was worth more than the company's value as a whole. He therefore proposed to acquire the company and to sell off many of its nontire businesses.

The Goldsmith offer provoked a grassroots resistance by union members, salaried employees, and retirees. These individuals were joined by plant communities and state and federal legislators. Goldsmith retreated.

The company, which had incurred significant debt in

fending him off, divested itself of its aerospace and automotive wheel operations to reduce its debt. But even these divestitures did not completely solve the problem. In June 1991, Goodyear's board brought in Stan Gault as CEO and charged him with accelerating the debt reduction process.

Gault moved aggressively to strengthen Goodyear's financial condition. Key elements of his strategy were debt reduction through divestitures, enhanced customer focus, aggressive marketing of new products, a total quality culture (TQC), and succession planning. His efforts produced fruit within roughly a year, and the general business community and peers began singing his and Goodyear's praises.

It was at this point that the concepts of seamlessness and the Morehouse course emerged. The Morehouse College experience is discussed later in this chapter.

Goodyear executives did not decide to foster seamlessness out of distress over the company's economics or competitive posture. They did so, instead, in the context of continuous improvement.

The total quality culture that Gault promoted, with its emphasis on teams, was having effect. As executives noted and celebrated progress in strengthening their competitive and economic standings under the leadership of their CEO, they delighted in how well the teaming process was working.

This success with teams and other quality processes, as well as Goodyear's improving financial position, led then Executive Vice President Frank Tully and Vice President Mike Burns to explore ways to rachet up the corporation's implementation of total quality culture. Tully realized that a strong focus on workforce diversity could facilitate TQC, and he also wanted to integrate the succession-planning work that was already under way.

As Tully and Burns pondered how to rachet up TQC, they envisioned an educational experience—not unlike one Goodyear had held at a major university some years before—that would allow the company's executives to explore the relationships among TQC, Managing Diversity, and succession planning. They wanted the exploration to be seamless, with the interrelationships prominent. The two executives desired an exploratory experience that would hasten the achievement of mutual adaptation with respect to Goodyear's strategic mixture. They were convinced that the synergy created by a seamless managerial philosophy would promote Goodyear's movement with TQC.

Tully and Burns believed that Goodyear was in the midst of a culture change, and that conducting the exploration in a traditional university setting would not affirm the transformation that was under way. They decided, instead, to hold the sessions at a leading historically black college. Morehouse College was selected.

Goodyear's Multistrategy Philosophy

The basic components of Goodyear's strategic diversity mixture are total quality culture, Managing Diversity, succession planning, and The Learning Company.

TOTAL QUALITY CULTURE (TQC). This process combines many of Goodyear's existing quality programs under one umbrella with new methodology and a strong customer focus. The *TQC mission* is "constant improvement in products and services to meet our customer's needs. This is the only means to business success for Goodyear and prosperity for its investors and associates."

At Goodyear, TQC has four guiding principles:

1. Customer satisfaction
2. Continuous process improvement
3. Dedication to people
4. Taking action on facts in a blame-free atmosphere

Supporting these guiding principles are four *essential elements*, vital components in the quality culture:

1. *Leadership.* Goodyear executives are driving the changes toward total quality culture. They have the responsibility to talk and walk the talk.
2. *Involvement.* TQC requires the intense, committed involvement of people. Goodyear seeks to achieve this in large part through team activities. Teams have been instrumental in generating ideas and in sharing them through presentations that serve as both communications and recognition vehicles.
3. *Products and processes.* Managers begin with an understanding of customer needs, then use a variety of quality tools and procedures to refine production processes. Among these tools and procedures are organizational development, baseline uniformity, statistical process control, supplier quality data systems and quality management systems.
4. *Education and training.* Goodyear began its push toward TQC with education and training, and continues this thrust as an integral part of the process. Reportedly, two-thirds of Goodyear's associates participate in some form of quality training each year.

MANAGING DIVERSITY. In the late 1980s, Goodyear executives committed to moving forward with workforce diversity. At the time, the leading-edge view of diversity was the process known as Managing Diversity (MD), which, as you read in Chapter 5, is specific to the workforce but often has the effect of pushing diversity thinking outward. By the time of the Morehouse experience, the company had initiated three major thrusts: (1) a series of conceptual briefings to senior human resources professionals, to Goodyear's chairman and president, and to senior Goodyear executives; (2) a cultural audit to unearth Goodyear's culture and systems; and (3) ongoing major MD educational efforts.

Goodyear's MD goal is "to leverage the diversity of all our associates so as to increase our global competitiveness." The company has defined MD as the "process of creating and maintaining an environment that naturally enables all associates to reach maximum potential in pursuit of organizational objectives."

The company has identified certain elements that must be in place to assure that Managing Diversity is possible:

- Equal expectations of associates on similar jobs
- No stereotyping of individuals
- Informing associates about the business
- Sensitivity to self-bias
- Education on diversity issues
- Recognition and measurement systems for MD
- Training for MD

Goodyear's executives believe that achieving these MD objectives will facilitate achievement of the company's broader objectives. These objectives are to:

- Gain a competitive advantage in the global marketplace
- Have all associates acquire a better understanding and respect for the differences in our diverse workforce
- Provide a work environment where all associates have an opportunity to reach their maximum potential
- Maximize productivity by leading, empowering, assisting, and motivating the associates of our diverse workforces
- Facilitate a change in our corporate culture and management styles
- Reinforce the respect and dignity for each associate for the skills and experience they bring to the workplace
- Promote the development of a diverse talent pool that will lead Goodyear into the twenty-first century.

It is worth pointing out that even though the diversity element of Goodyear's multipronged approach is the narrower form of Managing Diversity, the very fact that the company has constructed this mixture of strategies is in itself a manifestation of the broader Diversity Management. Not to put too fine a point on it, by embracing this mixture, they are moving toward Diversity Management, even though they do not call it so.

SUCCESSION PLANNING. This approach, introduced as a formal philosophy by CEO Stan Gault, was seen as critical to identifying and developing Goodyear's leaders for the near and distant future. As practiced at Goodyear, succession planning involves more than identifying quality candidates in the pipeline. It requires managing performance as well.

The first objective of the approach is to achieve an end state where each associate is performing all job responsibilities effectively. The second is to develop associates who show high potential by performing all their assigned job responsibilities and more. The third objective is to minimize the number of individuals with performance gaps.

THE LEARNING COMPANY. In contrast to the other philosophies, The Learning Company (TLC) gained in prominence as the company and its consultants moved forward with developing the Morehouse course. Goodyear managers had been placing emphasis on education and training, but they had not quite committed themselves to fostering collective organizational learning.

When the design team concluded that Goodyear's past practices would not necessarily be sufficient for future success and that the corporation's environment would become increasingly complex, it became clear that an individual *and* collective learning capability would be needed.

The Learning Company was defined as "an organization that facilitates, through experiences or study for all its members, the acquisition of knowledge, comprehension or mastery to continuously transform itself." To be a Learning Company is to adopt a way of life—a way of thinking and operating. A Learning Company has an organizational capability to sense environmental change and to make adjust-

ments as necessary and appropriate. At the same time, it insti-
tutionalizes where it can and remains fluid where its
environment dictates.

The Morehouse Course

Once Tully, Burns, and their colleagues decided what they
wanted to do, they approached three external organizations
for help. The organizations agreed to participate, and Morehouse College officials were delighted to serve as host.

With outside assistance identified and on board, a course
design team was formed, made up of Goodyear staff and
people from the outside organizations. The team held several
initial meetings where members learned about each other
and the perspectives each represented. Team members, who
had been charged with achieving a seamless point of view,
had first to work through the varied personalities and perspectives that their differences presented. They persevered
and evolved a framework for the course.

COURSE FRAMEWORK. After much discussion and debate,
the design team hypothesized that to achieve long-term success, Goodyear must have the following elements in place:

- *A strategic perspective*—an awareness of what is necessary to gain competitive advantage
- *A strong orientation toward learning*—a continued state
  of alert regarding environmental changes and their implications for organizational culture and systems
- *Committed associates*—people who base their actions on
  an internalized commitment to Goodyear's mission, vision, and strategy, rather than react to external controls
- *Successful multifunctional business teams*—effective communication, collaboration, and coordination across
  functions at the levels where the requisite knowledge
  and information are located
- *A high degree of organizational and individual compe-*

tence—individuals as well as organizational culture, systems, and practices affirm the desired behavior
- *A cultural renewal process*—a willingness and capability to modify corporate culture as dictated by environmental requirements

OPPORTUNITIES FOR SYNERGY. Among the four strategies around which the course would be built—total quality culture, Managing Diversity, succession planning, and The Learning Company—the design team noted many synergistic opportunities that could serve as a foundation for natural adaptation. Individually and collectively, these opportunities highlighted the need for seamlessness. Among them:

- *All require empowerment management.* Stated differently, all call for significant changes in managerial behavior. Each approach assumes that empowerment is a legitimate option for managers.
- *All require cultural change.* No corporation, especially one whose managers see it as an institution, can move forward with either the survival or business modes without changing the culture.
- *Managing Diversity, succession planning, and The Learning Company are all implicit in total quality culture.* TQC calls for engaging all associates in pursuit of corporate objectives. If associates are diverse, then MD becomes a prerequisite for fully realizing TQC. Similarly, the notions of understanding and responding to customer requirements, of seeking continuous improvement, and of taking action on facts all presume a learning capability. Finally, succession planning—with its emphasis on performance management, empowerment, and development—is essential to ensuring the managerial leadership required for TQC. Succession planning, as defined at Goodyear, becomes a major vehicle for evolving the empowerment management capability required for TQC.

- *MD fosters a Learning Company capability.* Collective learning presumes associates who are engaged and committed individually and collectively in pursuit of common organizational goals. This condition is a prerequisite for The Learning Company and the objectives of Managing Diversity.
- *MD enhances the capability to do succession planning.* MD, with its call for fully using all associates, legitimizes the requirement that managers "manage" (empower) the performance of all associates—not just the 20 percent who do 80 percent of the work.
- *Likewise, SP enhances the MD capability.* The more managers understand the processes, procedures, and tools of SP, the more they see *how* movement can be made in fully using all associates as called for by MD.
- *SP reaffirms the need for The Learning Company.* In the absence of individual and organizational learning, performance management (improvement) is most difficult. Managers who accept the need to foster the performance of all associates quickly see the importance of becoming a Learning Company.
- *The Learning Company provides the context that enables progress with TQC, MD, and SP.* Without a learning capability, all of the other philosophies are greatly compromised.
- *All of the philosophies focus on the need for individual* and *organizational capability.* Individual capability is needed in all four approaches, but there also must be organizational capability (culture and supporting systems and practices) to ensure sustainable natural progress. The philosophies must be built into the fiber of the organization.

Clearly, opportunities for achieving beneficial synergy existed in quality and quantity, and confirmed that mutual adaptation was a viable option.

COURSE FORMAT AND CONTENT. The course, held at More-house College, was five days long and accommodated twenty-five participants. In all, approximately 180 of Good-year's most senior managers attended.

Initial sessions focused on environmental change, a model of organizational evolution (see Chapter 3), and an introduction to succession planning. Participants then explored Managing Diversity, the concepts of leadership and management, and the doer and empowerment managerial models. They also worked in small groups to examine the corporation's mission, vision, strategy, and culture. The curriculum then turned to The Learning Company and the attributes of an effective learning organization.

Next came a "leader-to-leader" experience, where Goodyear executives were matched with Morehouse students interested in leadership. After an ice-breaker exercise, the student and the executive spent the remainder of the afternoon and the evening together. They were free to do whatever they wanted: campus tours, dinner at a restaurant or a student's apartment, visits to historic landmarks, and movies. While pursuing these options, they discussed backgrounds (differences and similarities) and leadership issues. All reported finding the experience educational, productive, and enjoyable.

Participants looked next at TQC in the context of The Learning Company, succession planning, and Managing Diversity. The focus then turned to the specifics of how the succession planning that was under way would be affecting Goodyear participants. Participants met without facilitators to plan their last day's agenda. Typically, they divided the day between a meeting without the facilitators and a question-and-answer period with them.

COURSE DYNAMICS. With few exceptions, the entire design team attended all sessions. Team members felt that their continuing presence would help facilitators to model and convey the concepts of mutual adaptation and seamlessness, and would enhance the perception that they were part of an integrated whole.

The design team's effort to model the learning organization affected the course's dynamics as well. Team members collectively and individually sought daily feedback and used it as the basis for day-to-day modifications. Between-session refinements were continuous. As each five-day experience ended, design team members/facilitators recognized once again how much their individual and collective thinking had evolved as a result of this process.

Team members encouraged participants to explore and play with concepts—to stretch their typical thought patterns. The intent was to create a mini learning community, a community of people who collectively explore alternative ways of thinking and their implications. There are no right or wrong answers in such a community. Ambiguity, complexity, ambivalence, and uncertainty abound. These realities disturbed Goodyear executives, who were largely doer managers. Their desire for concrete "to do" lists created ongoing diversity tension for design team members. At issue: whether to give in to the doer managers in the interest of "satisfying customer needs" or to persevere with the stretch agenda.

The design team used a kaleidoscope as an overarching symbol, and this played an important part in the course as well. Each manager was given an individual kaleidoscope; each part of the kaleidoscope was assigned a different meaning.

The body tube symbolized Goodyear, and the three mirrors represented the stakeholders (customers, associates, and shareholders) of the Business framework. The rotatable container represented dynamic environmental constraints within which organizational decisions are made. Picture fragments reflected different elements of Goodyear's business and environment. An arrow, for example, stood for leadership; a heart represented committed associates. At different points, team members/facilitators distributed picture fragments. The more pieces, the greater the pattern possibilities as one rotated the container. A third critical dynamic of the course was the introspection and reflection participants were encouraged to do. At strategic points, facilitators allowed time for journal entries, and they also urged participants to give significant thought to completing the daily feedback forms.

COURSE LEARNINGS. What did the executives take away? One learning centered around the concept of evolutionary framework (Institutional, Survival, or Business as discussed in Chapter 3). Reports indicate that some managers, when making decisions, are now seeking to identify the framework in which they are acting. To the extent that this is happening, a major course objective was achieved.

Many left with a greater understanding of succession planning and some of its processes. Goodyear has actively been expanding its efforts in this arena. Practical realities dictated that participants pay special attention to this topic.

For many, interacting with the students was an enormous personal learning experience. It gave them a chance to get to know young, bright, focused, primarily black-male students. As participants learned about the students, they learned about themselves and their corporation.

Some executives gained a greater understanding of Goodyear's strategic position. Most important, they left with an appreciation of the strategic consequences of being in the Institutional as opposed to the Business mode, given the dynamic, complex environment facing Goodyear. A consensus emerged that Goodyear would need considerable work to attain strategic clarity.

The dearth of clarity became apparent during an exercise calling for identification of Goodyear's strategic factors; participants typically came up with several items, many of them critical (necessary for viability) but not sources of competitive advantage.

Significant learnings emerged around leadership and management as well. Most sessions concluded that Goodyear executives were more managers than leaders and that this was reason for concern. Participants agreed that Goodyear managers were, by and large, doers and not empowerers. Several managers acknowledged their own doer status and saw the need for change, but expressed uncertainty as to how to make the shift.

The substantial attention given to understanding Goodyear's culture was also rewarded. Each group of participants came to the critical conclusion that Goodyear's culture works against transformation from the Institutional to the Business framework. Nearly all of the small group analyses identified the "family root" (relationships should be like those of a family) as a major aspect of Goodyear's culture. This root gives rise to practices more appropriate for the Institutional mode.

A major learning for many was the limited extent to which Goodyear executives perceived themselves to be empowered. As a result, some participants concluded that the corporation's culture not only discouraged the changes they had described as necessary but made it unlikely that they would be able to contribute to the needed culture change.

Finally, the course gave birth to an emerging sense of the interrelationships among the components of Goodyear's strategic diversity mixture, as well as the concept of mutual adaptation. Whether these beginnings will evolve into a full-blown, operational, integrated, managerial philosophy remains to be seen. Without doubt, however, the process has been launched.

Participant comments on leadership, management, and empowerment might at first glance appear to reflect negatively on Goodyear and its executives. But this is not so. Goodyear is a proud corporation with outstanding accomplishments. Its executives are competent individuals with admirable track records. The comments reflect what one would expect when bright, capable people struggle to escape the grips of the once eminently appropriate but increasingly inadequate Institutional framework.

Skepticism and ambivalence are natural consequences of institutionalization and are to be expected of managers coming to grips with developing a multistrategy philosophy and talking and thinking complexly. Managers at "institutional" corporations around the country are either going through their own soul searching, are on the verge of doing so, or are in dire need of undertaking an experience similar to that of the Morehouse participants.

In sum, Morehouse course participants left stimulated, thoughtful, and aware of the strategic challenges facing Goodyear. But they also left confused about what could or should be done. This is to be expected when companies move from the Institutional or Survival to the Business framework. Ideally, this awareness and confusion will set the stage for future mutual adaptation and progress toward seamlessness.

When the design team first met after the course, an intense debate focused on how much Goodyear really had changed. One school of thought argued that the corporation had changed greatly and was totally different; another conceded that major change had taken place, but believed that the roots (culture) remained unchanged. As the team interacted with Goodyear executives, the appreciation for changes made deepened significantly, but this appreciation was coupled with an awareness of the relatively unchanged mindsets and roots.

Lessons Learned

From the Goodyear experience several implications can be gleaned for others contemplating the pursuit of seamlessness to facilitate the shift to the Business framework.

1. Mutual adaptation toward seamlessness begins with changing the mindset, and this is not easy. Our mind is such an intimate place that we declare it off-limits to others and often to ourselves. As a result, we tend to lock out the possibility of change. But with permanent white water it is necessary to check mindsets for mid-course modifications. One

mindset is not likely to carry either an individual or a corporation through a lifetime.

A major challenge to mindset shifting is the practice in doer climates of defining mindsets as "soft" and refusing to acknowledge that examining them is a legitimate activity. If nothing else, Morehouse said to the Goodyear participants, "Check what is in your mind, for whatever is in there filters your perceptions and understanding of environmental realities."

2. Genuine mindset shifting can occur only where people are serious about achieving this objective. This seriousness and intensity can be promoted by an understanding of environmental realities and strategic implications. Without this context, any mindset shifting is academic play. It becomes real only when linked to business viability. True change (as opposed to pseudotransformation) brings with it commitment and a greater chance for naturally sustainable progress.

3. Financial data don't necessarily provide the best indications of transformation. Financial improvements can occur without mindset or root changes. A more reliable measure of transformation is the extent to which managers fully internalize the multistrategy philosophy and reflect it in their behavior.

4. When we—as individuals or corporations—go against our natural inclinations, we must be prepared to live with the tension that inevitably follows. The more corporations are able to change roots (culture), the less tension there will be. Whether individuals can change their basic inclinations remains an open question; the answer may depend on who the individual is. This is why the notion of organizational capability is so powerful. A culture and supporting systems may help people as they work to act against their inclinations.

A major learning for the design team was that organizational mindsets can be in one framework while associates' mindsets are in another. Associates, for example, can be in

Survival, while the organization is in Business. Here, the managerial task is to ensure that the organizational mindset is congruent with the environment. This will facilitate the transformation of individuals who are open to learning, and they in turn can help to ease (but not eliminate) the tension for those who cannot.

10

What Do I Do Next?
Case Study: General Motors

In the nine previous chapters of this book, we have undertaken together a challenging intellectual journey. It involves no less than rewriting what we mean by a basic term in common usage: *diversity*. That redefinition in itself is a very big change, but for our journey it was only the beginning.

We moved on to assemble, chapter by chapter, the Diversity Management process—a way of thinking about diversity and a way of using it in designing major corporate strategies. Through the chapters of Part One, you learned how to recognize diversity mixtures whenever and wherever they appear in various aspects of your organization. You also learned the eight action options of the Diversity Paradigm, which is the centerpiece of the Diversity Management process, and gained some practice in applying it.

As you read the experience of major corporations in the earlier chapters of Part Two (the General Motors story appears in this final chapter), you observed actual business situations through the lens of the Diversity Management process. These experiences served us as a laboratory for learning more about the process and providing additional practice in its application.

The question now becomes, what do I do next? That depends. It depends on where you are with all this, and where you wish to go.

If you are intrigued by the Diversity Management process and its implications but have not yet decided you wish to proceed further, your next step should be to play with the process for a while. Whenever the right situation presents itself, practice applying the process and the Paradigm; keep experimenting until you are able to make a definitive decision to proceed or not to proceed.

Or you may believe you are already comfortable with the process and are ready to proceed. My recommendation may come as a surprise: Don't. At least not yet. I recommend that you continue experimenting until Diversity Management becomes a way of life, second nature. Once you have *internalized* the process, you will be poised to serve as a change agent for your organization.

Or perhaps you have moved to the point where you already use the process on a daily basis as a framework for action and want to see it used more broadly in the rest of your organization. If so, I recommend moving forward in a structured way as a change agent. More about this later.

To put the issue a bit differently, if you decide that the Diversity Management process has merit and you want to see it put in place in your organization, you are by definition calling for change and putting yourself forth as the agent of that change. So your own answer to the question of "what next?" may be directed at either yourself or your company: "I, or we, have to make some changes."

In any event, whether the focus is on the individual or the organization, making change involves three tasks:

1. Talking the talk—gaining conceptual clarity
2. Thinking the talk—internalizing the process through experimentation and initial application to daily realities
3. Walking the talk—advancing to broad, in-depth application

The Individual Level

After ten years of working with individuals and organizations, I have concluded that people will have difficulty promoting organizational change unless they themselves have thoroughly internalized in their own behavior the change that they would like to see the company make. Once they do that, they have conceptual clarity about the content of the change as a whole. They also are found using the ingredients of the new process in their daily lives, both personal and professional.

This degree of clarity, together with daily practice, gives them an intimacy and familiarity that simultaneously motivates them and enhances their credibility. Without motivation and credibility based on knowledge and personal experience, the would-be change agent will be ill prepared for an uphill challenge. And let's face it, promoting a conceptually new approach such as the Diversity Management process is a major change and likely to be a difficult challenge.

How does a person gain conceptual clarity and internalize the process as a way of life? Let's begin with conceptual clarity.

Talking the Talk

At a minimum, you should seek clarity on the definitions associated with the Diversity Management process, and also on the differences between this and other, more familiar approaches such as Managing Diversity, affirmative action, and understanding differences. To reach this level of clarity, the following guidelines can help.

- *Take enough time.* This may seem trivial, but I assure you it is not. Some people are unwilling to take the time they need to secure clarity, primarily because they are not ready to make the minimum commitment. So as you approach the clarification process, ask yourself whether you are willing to make the necessary time commitment. If not, pursue readiness by exploring the possible benefits of committing. If such an exploration does not produce readiness, postpone your search for clarity until you are sufficiently motivated. There is no substitute for the commitment of time. Without it, you are unlikely to be successful.

▪ *Expose yourself to multiple presentations of the concepts.* This is necessary not because the concepts themselves are so difficult, but because they require a major mindset shift from our traditional ways of thinking. Departing from tradition is seldom easy.

Multiple presentations come through repetitions and also multiple vehicles. Repetition has its place. I've often heard managers say that they have listened to a presentation or attended a seminar more than once, and that each time they picked up significant learnings. Also, experiencing the concept from different angles through different media, such as presentations, videos, dialogue with colleagues, seminars, books, and articles, can facilitate clarification.

▪ *Teach the concepts.* No experience produces learning like teaching. I remember starting out as a college instructor teaching accounting and economics, and learning more about those topics as a teacher than I ever did as a student. Whom should you teach? Your spouse, perhaps. Often managers have commented, "Last night my husband and I were talking about how the concept related to something we're dealing with right now in our family. It was a very fruitful discussion."

Especially rewarding and challenging would be teaching the concept to people who have had little exposure to diversity issues, such as your neighbors, fellow members of social or professional clubs, or friends from your church or synagogue. Their lack of familiarity offers rich possibilities for learning. You might want to teach coworkers, either your direct reports or your peers, through brown-bag lunch discussions. You also could serve as a teacher to your boss.

• *Debate the concepts.* Search out people who are not likely to buy in to the concepts and engage them in *constructive* debate. Properly positioned as a learning experience, this exchange can be fruitful.

Similarly, be on the lookout for people whose terminology suggests conceptual confusion. Symptoms of such confusion are comments like the following: "Diversity is good." "Diversity is divisive." "Diversity means doing something for minorities and women." "We're doing diversity." Engage these people in constructive debate, and you likely will learn in the process.

I emphasize that this conceptual clarity is essential for effectiveness as a change agent, and that there is no shortcut to securing this understanding. For most of us, clarification calls for substantial involvement and commitment of energy and time.

Thinking the Talk

Talking and walking the talk may not be easy to do, but they are easy to understand. Thinking the talk is often overlooked altogether, yet it is critical to success.

Managers who think the talk make the Diversity Management philosophy a part of their ongoing thinking. They use the philosophy as a mental and conceptual template. Incoming data is filtered through it, and analyses and action planning are conducted within the context of it.

Internalization is the process of understanding the concepts as they relate to your daily lives. While ideally this understanding would be reflected in both your personal and professional lives, I believe that the greatest opportunity for initial internalization rests with the personal. Most of us hold personal issues dear. Having a work-originated mindset shift to aid us with personal matters would be an unexpected bonus and thus a potentially enormous opportunity for internalization.

To achieve this internalization, your first step in this phase is to identify the key diversity mixtures in your life, those with the greatest potential for affecting the quality of your life. They might include mixtures of the various roles you assume, career options, financial decisions, and the many people in your life: friends, club associates, etc. Your Diversity Management task is to address these mixtures in a manner that maximizes their contributions to your personal objectives.

The next question for each key mixture is, how have I addressed these personal mixtures in the past? Try to identify which action options you have relied upon for each mixture. Then ask yourself what gains were achieved by using those options, and what remains unresolved.

Then consider the crucial questions: Do you think the Diversity Management process would generate options for addressing the remaining issues? Do you get from the process insights that will take you beyond where you would be without Diversity Management? In other words, does the process add value for you?

This added-value aspect is critical. The clearer the value added, the greater your motivation will be to use and internalize the process and eventually to advocate its application in your organization. Without this internalization, you will not be ready to act as an agent for change.

Can you talk the talk and not think it? Certainly. Indeed, this is not only possible but quite common. This is seen, for example, in the manager who routinely talks teaming but thinks leadership. Operating from the "great man" model, he expects subordinates to bring all challenges to him for his personal attention. It is seen in the senior manager who advocates empowerment but expects direct reports to follow his directions and clone his behaviors. In institutions with stable environments, little need has existed to focus on this area. As a result, many managers have little or no experience with addressing, let alone changing, either their own or their subordinates' ways of thinking.

Walking the Talk

At this juncture, you regularly and routinely are using Diversity Management. Almost without conscious intent, you are identifying diversity mixtures in your personal and professional lives and drawing on Diversity Management as a framework for action in approaching the mixtures.

When you walk the talk, your actions demonstrate your words. If, for example, you are working within the context of an empowerment philosophy, your daily interactions with subordinates reflect empowerment.

In this phase, and *only* this phase, you are using Diversity Management in the full sense of the process. In talking the talk and thinking the talk, you are only preparing to use the process. This is a distinction not fully understood. Many cite activities related to talking and thinking as evidence that they are walking the talk. For example, people who take seminars on diversity often say, "We're doing diversity," implying that they are using the Diversity Management process. The reality, however, is that they are only preparing to use it. Talking and thinking are not walking, but only a means to that end.

As an aside, I should say that most corporations do not foster this personal application of Diversity Management. So, often even the most ardent advocates of Diversity Management in the organization lack an understanding of the diversity realities of their personal lives. A failure to facilitate such awareness and understanding hampers change at the individual *and* organizational levels.

The three components—talking, thinking, and walking the talk—constitute a diversity mixture in themselves. Managers who have the greatest success in dealing with complex environments will be skilled in all three. Those who are effective at one or two can find understanding and guidance in the Diversity Management process.

Managers who are good at talking the talk but weak on

thinking and walking will be seen as talking a good game but having poor follow-through. Visionary managers, good at thinking but poor on talking or walking, will have difficulty imbuing their organizations with their vision and will be ineffective in acting on this vision. Action-oriented managers who have the internal consistency that produces actions consistent with the complexity of the environment but who keep this information to themselves will provide insufficient leadership to sustain organizational transformation. Managers who are excellent at walking, moderately effective at talking, and inept at integrated thinking will seem busy and motivated. But the question will arise, but at what and motivated for what?

Which combination is preferred? Without a doubt, simultaneous proficiency in all three is optimal. Which are most likely? I suspect two are common: the talker of the talk who fades away because he can't walk or think it, and the visionary who thinks clearly but cannot move forward on her vision.

An interesting question is whether one can walk the talk without talking or thinking it. The answer is yes. This is the manager who walks by the direction of others but has limited understanding of the talk or interest in talking the talk. This manager often says, "Just tell me what you want me to do and let me get on with it."

What hinders managers' ability to simultaneously demonstrate all three skills? One limitation is lack of practice and subsequent lack of ability. Most institutional managers will need intensive coaching to be able to talk, think, and walk the talk. Few action-oriented managers are prepared to provide this level of coaching. A second barrier is the relative lack of legitimacy that action-oriented managers give to talking and thinking. Walking the talk reflects the management aspect of managing; talking and thinking the talk reflect its leadership aspects. Action managers are only beginning to give leadership its due.

The Organizational Level

Once you have achieved conceptual clarity, internalized the process, and put Diversity Management into operation as a part of your daily routine, as a way of life, you are ready to consider changing your organization toward Diversity Management.

The biggest barrier to leading that change is that most managers do not see talking and thinking activities as legitimate. They prefer to get to doing—walking—as soon as possible. In reality, sustained walking is not possible without first talking and thinking.

Robert L. Davis has articulated "A Framework for Change"[1] that the individual can use as a context for organizational change after first experiencing personal internalization. I will use a modified version of Davis's approach to convey how an organization can talk the talk, think the talk, and walk the talk.

Talking the Talk

Talking the talk involves communication. Senior managers must articulate the philosophy and its supporting rationale to everyone else. This articulation is a major vehicle for imbuing the philosophy throughout the organization and facilitating the buy-in and commitment of all managers and employees.

Talking the talk is not as straightforward as it may seem, especially for managers accustomed to the Institutional framework. Asking them to address the philosophy is a stretch. Asking them to articulate and sell it to organizational members can represent an enormous challenge. This reality has nothing to do with their absolute intellectual capabilities. It is related, instead, to a learned disability as the result of being successful in an institution.

The critical step in getting an organization to talk the talk is *education* (see Exhibit 10-1). I'm not referring to training, where the emphasis is on skill building and behavior modifi-

Exhibit 10-1. The preparation process for diversity management: talking and thinking the talk.

Tasks	Steps	Objectives	Desired Outcomes
TALKING THE TALK (*Gaining conceptual clarity*)	*Education* (*launching*)	• *Introducing the concepts*	• Diversity seen as the collective mixture • Motivation for diversity efforts understood • Role of culture understood
		• *Enroll stakeholders*	• Participants begin the *personal internalization* process • Diversity Management seen as a process • Roles understood • Participants commit themselves, time, and resources
		• *Develop organizational structure for implementation*	• Sponsor(s) and change agent(s) selected • Clarify reporting • Advisory group appointed • Elements of process agreed upon • Extent of education needs determined
THINKING THE TALK (*Relating to organizational realities*)	*Part 1: Strategic thinking session*	• *Relate Diversity Management to mission, vision, and culture*	• Importance of Diversity Management re: organization's mission, vision, strategy, and culture understood

(Continued)

Tasks	Steps	Objectives	Desired Outcomes
		• Conduct armchair audit	• Initial sense of the organization's culture achieved
		• Relate to strategic thrusts	• Synergistic relationships between Diversity Management and other thrusts understood
		• Make business case	• Viability significance of Diversity Management understood
		• Identify next preparation steps	• Clarity achieved as to next steps
	Part 2: Diagnosis (Cultural audit)	• Collect relevant data	• Interviews and focus groups completed • Employee survey completed • Archives search completed • Ethnographic data obtained
		• Infer cultural roots	• Interpretation team appointed • Data analyzed • Roots identified
	Part 3: Operational planning	• Do a gap analysis	• Current state (from diagnosis) compared with future state (from vision)

• Establish action priorities	• Nature of root and system changes determined • "Low-hanging fruit" selected • Priorities set for changing systems and roots • Education and training curricula developed
Part 4: *Operational* *implementation* *(collective* *internalization)*	
• Educate and train workforce	• Opportunity provided for senior leaders, supervisors and managers, and employees to learn new Diversity Management behaviors and skills
• Imbue new roots	• New behaviors and skills role modeled • Adoption of new behaviors and skills rewarded
• Modify systems as necessary	• System changes implemented and reinforced with rewards
Part 5: *Monitoring* *(preparation)*	
• Measure progress	• Measurements identified and assessed • Resurveys completed • Anecdotal data collected
• Raise the bar	• Higher objectives agreed upon
• Continuously improve	• Improvement opportunities identified and pursued

cation, but true education, defined as efforts to foster mindset shifts. Three types of education play a role here.

One type, *awareness education* is critical. This is the heart of your efforts to bring about conceptual clarity of Diversity Management throughout the organization. Only touching the bare essentials of the Diversity Management concept, awareness education can take many forms: public presentations, seminars, workshops, brown-bag lunch discussions, sessions around videotapes, books, or articles, and one-on-one sessions between individuals. Successful awareness education stimulates thought, not action.

A second type of education is *buy-in*. Your objective is to shift the mindsets of key organizational players to the point that they are willing to say, "Let's proceed with preparation for Diversity Management." This form of education goes deeper than awareness and relates to the strategic concerns of senior participants. Nevertheless, education of this kind still remains relatively shallow, in part because of the time constraints of senior officials.

The third type is *broad-base rollout*. Your objectives here are to encourage all employees to begin internalizing the ideas. This education is aimed at individuals below the managerial levels and so must be tailored to the particular needs of the various participants. The perspectives of your approach will vary, for example, as you address union members, participants in women's or minority networks, or employees located away from headquarters. Successful broad-base rollout leads people to awareness, an understanding that the concept can work for them, and a desire to operationalize Diversity Management in their personal and work lives.

To date, most organizations have focused on the managerial levels and have ignored the rank-and-file employees. You, however, cannot expect sustained progress without awareness and personal internalization at all levels.

If your educational efforts are successful, you will be able to put in place a structure for preparing for Diversity

Management. Specifically, you will be able to recruit individuals as sponsors, champions, advisers, and foot soldiers, and to clarify their roles and reporting relationships. This kind of structure is essential for the second phase of preparation, thinking the talk.

Thinking the Talk

To make the transition from only talking, to talking *and* thinking, a good vehicle is a *strategic thinking session* (see Exhibit 10-1). Successful sessions will enable participants to leave with an understanding about the relationship of Diversity Management to their organization's mission, vision, strategy, and culture; the synergy possibilities between Diversity Management and other strategic thrusts; the critical role of culture and system change; and specific next-step decisions. Strategic planning is the beginning point for collectively *internalizing* Diversity Management within a given organizational context.

Another "thinking" step is *diagnosis*. This step continues the process of examining Diversity Management within your organization; it involves ferreting out the basic assumptions that drive the organization and determining whether they will support Diversity Management progress. The diagnostic vehicle for this ferreting out is the cultural audit. This research-based process begins with the gathering of data about the operations of your organization as a way of fleshing out the "branches" of the cultural tree. Once you have determined the nature of the branches in detail, you infer from them the type of cultural roots (assumptions) that must be undergirding their viability. The final cultural-audit step is to determine whether the existing roots will hinder or facilitate Diversity Management. Although the cultural audit focuses primarily on culture, the data generated enable the same type of analyses with respect to the various organizational systems (resource allocation, planning, selection, measurement, rewards, and development). Your diagnostic results set the stage for planning how to internalize Diversity Management in your organization.

Operational planning, the third thinking step, seeks to specify where change is needed and to establish priorities. One good way to determine where change is needed is to conduct what is known as a gap analysis. Decide what conditions you'd like to see in place and compare those to the conditions that now exist, and the gap will dictate where change is required in terms of cultural roots and systems. In reality, you will find identifying the need for change relatively easy, compared to determining *how* to change. Leaders in one corporation have struggled for years over how to change, after agreeing on the need for change. Once clear about the how, you will find it helpful to establish priorities.

A major assumption at this stage is that you understand Diversity Management and know the type of behaviors and skills that will be required. In this step, you wish to identify what you must do to create an environment that will foster those behaviors and skills.

Operational implementation, the fourth thinking step, calls for you to begin the internalizing activities reflected in your operational plan. This means developing and training your workers, imbuing new cultural roots in the organization, and modifying systems as necessary. With respect to your workforce, it means fostering the continuing process of mindset shifting and personal internalization, and also adopting new Diversity Management skills and behavior. In particular you need to encourage all employees to internalize Diversity Management in their own individual experiences, both personal and work experiences.

As mindset shifts and personal internalization evolve, you begin to train employees in applying the Diversity Management approach and action options. Your goal is to help them develop skills in recognizing diversity mixtures, diagnosing contingencies, and applying the various action options.

Imbuing new cultural roots requires leadership from

you. You must articulate the new roots and their supporting rationales at every opportunity, over and over. You must make these new roots a critical point of departure in planning and evaluating the organization's efforts across the board. You must be prepared to do this personally for years—or if not, you must ensure that the organization develops enough leadership capacity that it is done by someone. Successfully embedding the new roots will require a sustained, ongoing effort.

Modification of systems, such as selection, measurement, development, and rewards, involves two phases: making the necessary changes and then reinforcing them. Reinforcement involves articulating the rationales in terms of mission, vision, and strategy, relating the changes to new and old roots, and offering formal and informal rewards that reaffirm the system changes.

The fifth and final thinking step is *monitoring*. Here, you continuously measure progress, raise expectations and improve performance. We must be clear that I am talking about monitoring your preparation efforts, not monitoring how well you are doing with Diversity Management per se.

One of your most crucial decisions will be identifying how you will measure progress. Some argue for making these decisions early on. I do not. Given that preparing for Diversity Management is new for most managers, I believe that measurement parameters should be identified and revised as you go along. For example, as you move from one thinking step to another, you specify the progress measures for each step in turn.

Once you have determined your measurement parameters, your next task is to gather the data needed for your assessments. Pull in everything, from both formal and informal sources. You must not fall into the trap of relying only on hard or soft data, or only on quantitative or qualitative. You need access to any kind of data that will enrich your assessments.

After your evaluations you should, in the spirit of continuous improvement, seek agreement on how to raise the bar. Your goal is continuous improvement, and you must continuously search for opportunities for improvement. The process, in other words, has no end. This reflects the reality that, although I have delineated the tasks in linear sequence, overlap and several iterations can be involved. There is not likely to be a one-time pass-through of the tasks.

Again, let me emphasize that through monitoring you are seeking to enhance your *preparation* for Diversity Management, not the doing of Diversity Management. After success with talking and thinking, you will be prepared for walking the talk, for applying the Diversity Management process. This is where many organizational leaders become confused. Given the time, energy, and financial costs involved in talking and thinking, many managers find it tempting to proclaim that by doing those early steps they are doing (or have done) diversity. The reality is that they have only prepared for doing it.

The magnitude of the talking and thinking tasks and also the confusion with walking explain why so few corporations have made substantial, sustainable progress with Diversity Management. Typically, they suspend talking and thinking before the organization has become sufficiently prepared, with the predictable result that little progress is achieved.

Walking the Talk

Walking the talk is your end goal. You want your organization collectively to be able to identify key diversity mixtures, diagnose related contingencies, and apply action options as dictated by those diagnoses. Achieving these objectives is made possible by the basic Diversity Management skills learned and practiced in thinking the talk, and by the culture and system changes put in place in the thinking steps. Together, they create a climate that can facilitate sustained walking.

Just as you did during the two preparation phases, during the application phase you must monitor progress and identify opportunities for improvement (see Exhibit 10-2). Except that it focuses on applications, monitoring the walking is the same as with talking and thinking.

Key to monitoring will be deciding how to measure progress. You should identify and develop measurements that give feedback on application of the basic Diversity Management skills. The emphasis clearly is on doing.

Conceivably, that feedback could highlight some weaknesses in your application, so you might find it necessary at some point to go back and forth between preparation and doing. Remember, the steps are not absolutely sequential. Even when you make substantial progress with preparation and shift your focus to doing, at some point you may have to return to the talking or thinking activities. The fact that Diversity Management is an embryonic process also increases the likelihood that you will have to go back and forth between preparation and doing. As the process is refined, managers will have to go back to talking and thinking to incorporate new developments. So continuous improvement in doing will require continuous improvement in preparation.

You may have noted that I have devoted a relatively small amount of space to discussing walking the talk. This contrasts with the real world, where managers frequently *talk* incessantly about walking the talk. The governing principle in our discussion here is that good preparation makes for easier doing; where ample attention has been given to talking and thinking, walking is relatively straightforward.

The biggest barrier to Diversity Management is that managers—either because of personal disinclinations or perceptions of time limitations—do not prepare sufficiently. Inadequate preparation greatly compromises the chances for success. Let's take a look at the experiences of one corporation that has made a commitment to preparation.

Exhibit 10-2. The process for applying Diversity Management: walking the talk.

Tasks	Steps	Objectives	Desired Outcomes
WALKING THE TALK (Applying the process)	Part 1: Application	• Identify key mixtures	• Key mixtures identified • Priorities established
		• Diagnose contingencies	• Contingency diagnosis completed for each key mixture
		• Apply action options as indicated by contingency diagnoses	• Actions taken as dictated by contingency diagnoses
	Part 2: Monitoring	• Measure progress	• Measurements identified and assessed • Resurveys completed • Anecdotal data collected
		• Raise the bar	• Higher objectives agreed upon
		• Continuously improve	• Improvement opportunities identified and pursued

The General Motors Story*

General Motors is a prime example of a corporation whose senior management has made a commitment to talking and thinking in preparation for doing, as opposed to rushing headlong into doing.

Diversity Context

General Motors is engaged in moving toward what it calls Managing Diversity, which it defines as "the process of creating and maintaining an environment that naturally enables General Motors employees, suppliers and communities to fully contribute in pursuit of total customer enthusiasm." You will recall from Chapter 5 that Managing Diversity is one element of Diversity Management. Indeed, the company's managers are beginning to think in terms of Diversity Management and, given their focus on mixtures other than the workforce, are likely to broaden their perspective. So the talking and thinking that have been done in preparation for Managing Diversity implicitly also has been preparation for Diversity Management. This is a case where a company's actions have been ahead of its labeling of them.

According to General Motors' definition of Managing Diversity, the aim of its MD process is to enable "employees, suppliers and communities to fully contribute in pursuit of total customer enthusiasm." This definition thus highlights two realities:

1. The corporation has incorporated Managing Diversity into its general strategic thrust toward total customer enthusiasm. And one of the fundamental principles of Diversity Management is that it is directly related to strategic issues.
2. By encompassing suppliers and communities as well

*This case is based on materials provided by General Motors Corporation.

as employees, General Motors defines diversity as being more than the workforce. Specifically, its managers also are addressing diversity mixtures related to its consumer base, its network of minority suppliers, and its community relations—in addition to its human resources.

In each of these target areas, objectives have been established:

Marketing (consumer base) objectives

- To develop cars and trucks that reflect the needs of diverse markets
- To optimize customer enthusiasm
- To use our internal intelligence of the diverse customer base to create products and services that will attract new customers and retain existing customers
- To increase profitable market share and volume

Human resources management objectives

- To attract, retain, develop, and advance the best talent
- To improve product quality
- To foster an environment that works for all
- To become an employer of choice among a diverse population

Minority-supplier development objectives

- To create a partnership relationship with minority suppliers
- To improve product quality
- To increase minority suppliers' share in the business opportunities within the General Motors community

Community relations objectives

- To increase awareness of General Motors' approach to managing diversity
- To enhance General Motors' image as a company that values diversity
- To become the automotive company of choice within the community

For all four target areas, General Motors is taking a three-prong approach: affirmative action, understanding differences, and Managing Diversity. Recent comments by CEO John F. Smith, Jr., reflect the corporation's multiprong approach:

> When it comes to Affirmative Action, we will continue to press the envelope, but at the same time we will be moving to a broader concept—that is, Managing Diversity. As a global company, we want to fully benefit from a diverse work force. Our commitment to diversity extends beyond the door of our company. It includes our dealerships, our suppliers, and the many communities where we operate.

In the area of human resources, GM is using affirmative action to create a diverse workforce and to promote upward mobility for minorities and women; understanding differences calls for mutual respect among diverse groups and increased receptivity of affirmative action; and Managing Diversity prescribes mindset shifts and system changes. For the marketing, supplier, and community relations mixtures, General Motors is beginning to interpret affirmative action, understanding differences, and Managing Diversity in the context of the Diversity Paradigm's action options.

As a way of organizing their pursuit of Managing Diversity in the target arenas, Bill Brooks, Vice President, Corporate Relations, and Vicky Jones, Director, Diversity Strategies, have adopted a change model from the corporation's total quality efforts; they call it the General Motors Common Process Model.

The Common Process Change Model

The Common Process Model presents the change process as five steps: (1) Identify; (2) Analyze, (3) Plan, (4) Implement, and (5) Evaluate. Exhibit 10-3 is a summary of this process.

What is particularly revealing for our purposes is the close parallels between this model and the talk/think/walk approach described earlier in this chapter. Take a look:

Identify◀------▶Talking the Talk—Education
                Thinking the Talk—Part 1: Strategic thinking session

Analyze ◀------▶Thinking the Talk—Part 2: Diagnosis (Cultural audit)

Plan ◀----------▶Thinking the Talk—Part 3: Operational planning

Implement◀-----▶Thinking the Talk—Part 4: Operational implementation

Evaluate ◀------▶Thinking the Talk—Part 5: Monitoring (Preparation)

So, we can say that the Common Process represents General Motors' approach to *preparing* for Diversity Management.

Actions to Date

Through the Common Process vehicle, General Motors seeks to do the talking and thinking necessary for creating an environment that will enable sustainable walking the talk (Diversity Management). And in that the company has made substantial progress.

STEP 1, IDENTIFY. Much has been done. Vice President Bill Brooks and an outside consultant have as a team made awareness presentations to most of General Motors' senior executives. The objectives of the presentations have been to foster

Exhibit 10-3. Managing Diversity: a Common Process Model for change.

Tasks	Objectives	Actions
1. IDENTIFY	• Build commitment to initiate change 　—Create understanding 　—Gain enrollment	• Develop ongoing education/awareness plan
	• Establish infrastructure to drive common process	• Build infrastructure 　—Define components of infrastructure 　—Fill key roles 　—Develop communication plan 　—Develop working vision statement 　—Identify linkages with existing strategies
	• Adopt and adapt common process	
2. ANALYZE	• Gain understanding of current culture (facilitating and hindering factors)	• Conduct cultural assessment 　—Survey the workforce 　—Archival search 　—Focus groups 　—Interviews 　—Customer input 　—Synthesis of data
3. PLAN	• Develop plan to close gap between current state and the vision	• Formalize vision • Identify systems that support and hinder achieving vision and practices (formal and informal) • Identify appropriate behavior to support change
4. IMPLEMENT	• Implement plan	• Utilize linkages with existing strategies • Modify systems and practices to support vision • Support leadership in articulating new roots
5. EVALUATE	• Continuous improvement	• Reassess culture, raise the bar, and implement change(s) as needed

understanding of the general conceptual framework, appreciation of diversity as a business issue and a potential source of competitive advantage, and an awareness of General Motors' particular diversity aspirations and the Common Process that will drive progress. Altogether, the two men have made more than forty presentations, typically four hours long, and these sessions have stimulated thoughtful questions and discussions. As part of the education process, General Motors' diversity leaders have also developed plans for broad-base rollout to rank-and-file managers and professional staff.

To reinforce conceptual awareness and clarity, General Motors has taken an innovative step. Corporate diversity leaders have recruited senior executives to serve as diversity champions for each major organizational unit. They are expected to advocate the importance of addressing diversity as a strategic issue. Supporting each champion is a diversity practitioner who accepts responsibility for developing and implementing the unit's Common Process activities. These practitioners from around the corporation also come together as The Diversity Partners. In these meetings, they share experiences, host practitioners from other corporations, discuss current diversity topics, and receive reports from subcommittees.

Plans exist for keeping the General Motors community informed of the corporation's diversity aspirations and progress toward achieving them. A diversity brochure detailing definitions, plans, and senior executive support was sent to everyone in the total corporation.

STEP 2, ANALYZE. Plans are now under way for moving to the second step. Diversity practitioners are preparing to conduct a cultural audit. In several organizational units, a critical aspect of the preparation has senior management going through an "armchair cultural audit." This process offers a series of exercises that give participants a preliminary feel for their organization's culture and how that culture might facilitate or hinder change.

Once the armchair audits are completed, managers will turn to solidifying plans for gathering data for the formal research-based cultural audit. The results will provide the basis for the third step of planning.

What Next?

I have sought to give a flavor of the diversity-oriented talking and thinking under way at General Motors. General Motors' leadership is deliberately avoiding rushing into action without appropriate preparation.

What can we expect in the future? General Motors will complete the cultural audit, use the data to develop plans for further preparation, and implement them along with an appropriate measurement process. In all probability, more than one iteration will be required before General Motors' managers will consider themselves ready to walk the talk. Only after this thorough preparation will General Motors be able to say it is "doing diversity management."

You might say this is a lot of preparation. Indeed, it is. This is necessary because Diversity Management goes against the grain of most organizations, where short-term action orientation is the order of the day. To be successful at something so new and seemingly radical, involving concepts so fundamental as cultural change and major mindset shifts, significant preparation is unavoidable. General Motors has provided a role model of how the early preparatory steps can be executed.

Notes

Preface

1. R. Roosevelt Thomas, Jr., *Beyond Race and Gender: Unleashing the Power of Your Total Work Force by Managing Diversity* (New York: AMACOM, 1991).

Chapter 1

1. Thomas, *Beyond Race and Gender*.

2. This definition and discussion of diversity can be found in R. Roosevelt Thomas, Jr., "A Diversity Framework," in *Diversity in Organizations: New Perspectives for a Changing Workplace*, Martin M. Chemers, Stuart Oskams, and Mark Costanzo, eds. (Thousand Oaks, Calif.: Sage Publications, 1995), pp. 318–319.

An earlier version of this material was presented as "The Diversity Paradigm" at the Diversity Group Symposium held at Morehouse College on February 9–10, 1994. The symposium was entitled "Managing Diversity: A Conceptual Framework."

3. Roland Calori, Gerry Johnson, and Philipps Sarnin, "CEOs' Cognitive Maps and Score of the Organization," *Strategic Management Journal*, vol. 15, no. 6 (1994), p. 437.

4. William B. Johnston and Arnold H. Packer, *Workforce 2000: Work and Workers for the 21st Century* (Indianapolis, Ind.: Hudson Institute, 1987).

5. Case studies of how teams are being used in organizations can be found in Richard S. Wellins, William C. Byham, and

George R. Dixon, *Inside Teams: How 20 World-Class Organizations Are Winning Through Teamwork* (San Francisco: Jossey-Bass Publishers, 1994).

6. John Naisbitt, *Global Paradox: The Bigger the World Economy, the More Powerful Its Smallest Players* (New York: William Morrow and Company, Inc., 1994).

7. Descriptions of "merger waves" are provided in Philip H. Mirvis and Mitchell Lee Marks, *Managing the Merger: Making It Work* (Englewood Cliffs, N.J.: Prentice-Hall, 1992), pp. 31–36.

8. Sue Shellenbarger, "So Much Talk, So Little Action," *Wall Street Journal*, June 21, 1993, pp. R1, R4, R6.

9. A conceptual model for dealing with relationships among functional subunits is offered in Paul R. Lawrence and Jay W. Lorsch, *Organization and Environment: Managing Differentiation and Integration* (Boston: Division of Research, Graduate School of Business Administration, Harvard University, 1967).

10. Peter B. Vail, *Managing as a Performing Art* (San Francisco: Jossey-Bass Publishers, 1989), pp. 1–32.

11. Paul R. Lawrence, Louis B. Barnes, and Jay W. Lorsch, eds., "Higgins Equipment Company (B)," in *Organizational Behavior and Administration: Cases and Reading* (Homewood, Ill.: Richard D. Irwin, 1976), pp. 325–336.

Chapter 2

1. Joel Arthur Barker, *Future Edge* (New York: William Morrow, 1992), p. 32.

2. Thomas, "A Diversity Framework," pp. 249–250.

Chapter 3

1. Carol J. Loomis, "Dinosaurs?" *Fortune*, May 3, 1993, pp. 36–42.

2. The model presented here is a modified version of one that framed a recent five-day seminar for Goodyear senior executives (see Chapter 9). In addition to myself, the team develop-

ing the model consisted of Steve Drotter of Drotter and Associates, Elizabeth Holmes of the Center for Creative Leadership, and from Goodyear: Mark Hartman, Karen Henry, and Jackie Taylor.

3. Loomis, "Dinosaurs?"

4. Vail, *Managing as a Performing Art.*

5. Johnston and Packer, *Workforce 2000.*

6. "Meet the New Consumer," *Fortune,* Autumn/Winter 1993, pp. 6–7.

7. "Relationship Investing," *Business Week,* March 15, 1993, pp. 68–75.

Chapter 4

1. Thomas, *Beyond Race and Gender,* pp. 46–47.

2. Ibid., p. 48.

3. Leonard R. Sayles refers to the involved empowerment manager as the "working leader." Leonard R. Sayles, *The Working Leader: The Triumph of High Performance Over Conventional Management Principles* (New York: The Free Press, 1993).

4. Kenichi Ohmae, *The Mind of the Strategist: Business Planning for Competitive Advantage* (New York: Penguin Books, 1982), p. 36.

5. Edgar H. Schein, *Organizational Culture and Leadership* (San Francisco: Jossey-Bass Publishing, 1985), pp. 1–22.

6. Thomas, *Beyond Race and Gender,* pp. 12–14.

7. What I refer to as "sources of meaning" corresponds to O. A. Ohman's "skyhooks." O. A. Ohman, " 'Skyhooks' With Special Implications for Monday Through Friday," *On Human Relations* (New York: Harper and Row, 1983), pp. 436–452.

Chapter 5

1. Thomas, *Beyond Race and Gender,* p. 21.

2. Ibid., pp. 21–22.

3. Ibid., p. 10.

4. Frederick R. Lynch, *Invisible Victims: White Males and the Crisis of Affirmative Action* (New York: Greenwood Press, 1989).

5. Stephen L. Carter, *Reflections of an Affirmative Action Baby* (New York: Basis Books, 1991).

6. Calori, Johnson, and Sarnin, "CEOs' Cognitive Maps."

7. An example of such a philosophy is Douglas McGregor's Theory Y assumptions. Douglas McGregor, *The Human Side of Enterprise* (New York: McGraw-Hill, 1985), pp. 45–57.

8. R. Roosevelt Thomas, Jr., "Managing the Psychological Contract," in *Organizational Behavior and Administration: Cases and Readings*, Paul R. Lawrence, Louis B. Barnes, and Jay W. Lorsch, eds. (Homewood, Ill.: Richard D. Irwin, 1976), pp. 465–480.

Chapter 6

1. This discussion of lifestyle issues is an expansion of a paper entitled "Managing Diversity and Work/Family Issues," prepared for an executive symposium co-sponsored by Aetna Life and Casualty and The Women's Legal Defense Fund. Held on April 7–8, 1993, the symposium focused on the theme: "Beyond Human Resources: The Business Case for Creating Flexible Work Environments."

2. Lotte Bailyn, *Breaking the Mold: Women, Men, and Time in the New Corporate World* (New York: The Free Press, 1993), pp. 3–4.

3. William H. Whyte, Jr., *The Organization Man* (New York: Simon and Schuster, 1956).

4. U.S. Department of Labor, *Report on the American Workforce* (Washington: GPO, 1994), p. 189.

5. Shellenbarger, "So Much Talk," p. R4.

6. Bailyn, *Breaking the Mold*, p. 6.

7. Laurie M. Grossman, "What About Us: Family Support Programs May Have a Side Effect: Resentment Among Childless Workers," *Wall Street Journal*, June 21, 1993, p. R8.

8. Ibid.

9. Ibid.

10. Ibid.

11. Thomas, *Beyond Race and Gender*, pp. 13–14.

12. Richard Tanner Pascal and Anthony G. Athos, *The Art of Japanese Management: Applications for American Executives* (New York: Simon and Schuster, 1981), p. 178.

13. Ohman, "'Skyhooks' With Special Implications," pp. 435–449.

14. Ibid., p. 445.

Chapter 7

1. Lawrence and Lorsch, *Organization and Environment*. These researchers compared departments in terms of formality of structure, interpersonal orientation, time orientation, and goal orientation.

2. John P. Kotter, "Organization Design," in *Organization Behavior and Administration*, Lawrence, Barnes, and Lorsch, eds., p. 487.

3. Examples would be the supervisor who integrates the subunits for which she is responsible, or the scheduling department that coordinates relationships between sales and marketing. "Organizing Human Resources in a Single-Business Company," in *Organization: Text, Cases, and Readings on the Management of Organizational Design and Change*, John P. Kotter, Leonard A. Schlesinger, and Vijay Sathe, eds. (Homewood, Ill.: Richard D. Irwin, 1979), pp. 123–124, 126–127.

4. Examples would be temporary or permanent task forces and teams composed of members of the subunits being integrated. Kotter, "Organization Design," p. 497.

5. Ibid., pp. 494–497.

6. Paul R. Lawrence and Jay W. Lorsch, *Developing Organizations: Diagnosis and Action* (Reading, Mass.: Addison-Wesley, 1969), pp. 24–26.

7. Stanley M. Davis and Paul R. Lawrence, *Matrix* (Reading, Mass.: Addison-Wesley, 1977), pp. 11–14.

8. Ibid., pp. 46–48.

9. Paul R. Lawrence, Harvey F. Kolodny, and Stanley M. Davis, "The Human Side of the Matrix," in *Organization*, Kotter, Schlesinger, and Sathe, eds., pp. 241–246.

10. Ibid., pp. 246–249.

11. Michael Hammer and James Champy, *Reengineering the Corporation: A Manifesto for Business Revolution* (New York: Harper Business, 1993), p. 32.

12. Ibid., p. 161.

13. Ibid., pp. 163–164.

14. Ibid., p. 162.

15. Ibid., p. 168.

Chapter 8

1. Christopher A. Bartlett and Sumantra Ghoshal, *Managing Across Borders: The Transnational Solution* (Boston: Harvard Business School Press, 1989), p. 51. Kenichi Ohmae, "Managing in a Borderless World," in *Going Global: Succeeding in World Markets* (Cambridge: Harvard University, 1991), p. 10. Theodore Levitt, "The Globalization of Markets," in *Going Global*, p. 18.

2. Illustrative of materials available are: J. Steward Black, Hal B. Gregerson, and Mark E. Mendenhall, *Global Assignments: Successfully Expatriating and Repatriating International Managers* (San Francisco: Jossey-Bass Publishers, 1962); Nancy Henderson, "Doing Business Abroad: The Problem of Cultural Differences," *Business American*, December 3, 1979, pp. 8–9; William J. Lederer and Eugene Burdick, *The Ugly American* (New York: W. W. Norton, 1958); A. H. Walle, "Beyond the Ugly American," *Management Decision*, vol. 28, no. 7 (1990), pp. 11–16.

3. Bartlett and Ghoshal, *Managing Across Borders*, p. 33.

4. Ibid., p. 137.

5. Ibid., pp. 199–200.

6. Ohmae, "Managing in a Borderless World," p. 10.

7. Bartlett and Ghoshal, *Managing Across Borders*, pp. 51–52.

8. Ibid., pp. 57–71.

9. Thomas, *Beyond Race and Gender*, pp. 50–59.

Chapter 9

1. Calori, Johnson, and Sarnin, "CEOs' Cognitive Maps," p. 437.

Chapter 10

1. Robert L. Davis, "A Framework for Change," working paper, The American Institute for Managing Diversity, 1993.

Index